Reading with Canadian Celebrities

Grades 4-8

Written by Ruth Solski

About the author:
Ruth Solski was an educator for 30 years. She has written many educational resources over the years and is the founder of S&S Learning Materials.
As a writer, her main goal is to provide teachers with a useful tool they can implement in their classrooms to bring the joy of learning to children.

Copyright © 2010

This publication may be reproduced under licence from Access Copyright, or with the express written permission of On The Mark Press / S&S Learning Materials, or as permitted by law.

All rights are otherwise reserved, and no part of this publication may be reproduced, stored in a retrieval system, or transmitted in any form or by any means, electronic, mechanical, photocopying, scanning, recording or otherwise, except as specifically authorized. "We acknowledge the financial support of the Government of Canada through the Book Publishing Industry Development Program (BPIDP) for this project."

All Rights Reserved
Printed in Canada

Published in Canada by:
S&S Learning Materials
15 Dairy Avenue
Napanee, Ontario
K7R 1M4
www.sslearning.com

ISBN: 9781554950898

SSJ1-78

At A Glance

Learning Expectations	Male Athletes	Female Athletes	Male Actors	Female Actors	Male Musicians	Female Musicians
Reading Comprehension						
• Locating information	•	•	•	•	•	•
• Using context clues	•	•			•	•
• Recalling events	•	•		•	•	•
• Evaluation	•	•		•		
• Sequential ordering	•	•	•		•	•
• Classifying information	•	•		•	•	•
• Identifying main idea	•			•		
• Locating proof	•	•	•	•		
• Understanding idioms	•					
• Recalling details		•	•	•	•	•
Vocabulary Development						
• Identifying phonetic sounds	•	•		•	•	
• Sentence ordering	•				•	
• Classifying words to meanings	•	•	•	•	•	•
• Identifying parts of speech	•			•	•	•
• Paragraph writing	•	•		•	•	
• Identifying syllables, compound words	•	•	•		•	•
• Identifying antonyms, synonyms, homophones	•	•	•	•	•	•
• Classifying words	•				•	•
Research Skills						
• Using the Internet to locate information	•	•	•	•	•	•
• Mapping skills					•	•

Reading with Canadian Celebrities

Table of Contents

At A Glance™ 2
About This Book 4

Biographies and Worksheets

Male Athletes

Wayne Gretzky 5
Kurt Browning 7
Donovan Bailey 9
Steve Nash 11
Bobby Orr 13
Lennox Lewis 15
Alex Baumann 17

Female Athletes

Cindy Klassen 19
Chantal Petitclerc 21
Perdita Felicien 23
Beckie Scott 25
Hayley Wickenheiser 27
Beth Underhill 29
Karen Cockburn 31

Male Actors

Mike Myers 33
Ryan Gosling 35
Michael J. Fox 37
Matthew Perry 39
Jim Carrey 41
Keanu Reeves 43
Kiefer Sutherland 45

Female Actors

Sarah Polley 47
Kim Cattrall 49
Neve Campbell 51
Sandra Oh 53
Wendy Crewson 55
Anna Paquin 57
Meg Tilly 59

Male Musicians

The Barenaked Ladies 61
Kalan Porter 63
Bryan Adams 65
Billy Talent 67
Sam Roberts 69
Brian Melo 71
Sum 41 73

Female Musicians

Avril Lavigne 75
Nellie Furtado 77
Celine Dion 79
Sarah McLachlan 81
Chantal Kreviazuk 83
Jully Black 85
Bif Naked 87

Answer Key 89

ISBN: 9781554950898  SSJ1-78

Reading with Canadian Celebrities

About this Book:

This resource is a compilation of forty-two biographies and forty-two worksheets that pertain to famous Canadian male and female athletes, actors, and musicians. The biographies have been created to promote and familiarize students with Canadians who have become famous in the fields of sport, music and drama while providing an interesting genre to strengthen students' reading skills. The worksheets that accompany the biographies focus on the development of a variety of reading comprehension skills, the development and reinforcement of vocabulary and language skills, and the continuing development of research skills.

Ways to Use the Biographies and Worksheets

1. **Reproducible Worksheets:** Reproduce each biography and worksheet and staple them together to form a handout. The students read the biography, discuss the information, and then complete the activities on the worksheet.

2. **Laminated Folders:** Each biography and its worksheet could be reproduced and glued to the inside of a file folder. A photograph of the male athlete obtained from a sports magazine, the newspaper or the Internet could be glued to the front of the file folder. Multiple folders on each athlete may have to be made depending on the size of the group or class.

Example: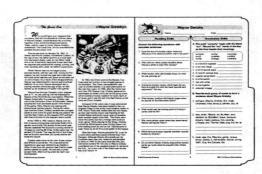

The file folders should be laminated to ensure longer usage. The folders could be placed at an Interest Centre in the classroom. Each student chooses a folder on one of the athletes, reads the biography, and records the answers on the worksheet in a notebook or workbook.

3. **Discussion Topics:**

   - Types of Sports
   - Types of Sporting Equipment
   - Sportsmanship
   - Types of Drama and Acting
   - Canadian Films and Movies
   - Characteristics of a good actor, athlete, musician
   - Survey and graphing popular musicians, athletes, actors, types of sports, kinds of music

   - Types of Musicians
   - Types of Music
   - Musical Instruments
   - Training requirements for an athlete, actor, musician
   - Advantages and disadvantages of being an actor, athlete, musician
   - How sports, acting and music have evolved.

The Great One — ★ Wayne Gretzky ★

Who would have ever imagined that a scrawny little kid from Brantford, with the name of Wayne Gretzky, would develop into a scoring machine in the world of professional hockey. Today, and for years to come, Wayne Gretzky, nicknamed 'The Great One,' will be considered the greatest hockey player ever.

Wayne was born on January 26, 1961, to Walter and Phyllis Gretzky in Brantford, Ontario. At the age of two, his father had him at a local park rink learning to skate. Later on, his father made him a rink in the family backyard. It was here that he acquired and practised his skating, scoring, and stick handling skills under his father's supervision.

When Wayne was six, he began to play peewee hockey with ten year olds. During his first season, he only scored one goal and cried when he found out he was the only player on the team not to win a trophy. As a result of this disappointment, Wayne was determined to improve and practised faithfully. In no time, Wayne developed into a scoring machine and at the age of ten, he had racked up an amazing 378 goals in 82 games.

Wayne flew through Canada's junior leagues and at 17, he was playing with the Indianapolis Racers of the World Hockey Association. When the Racers folded after five seasons, Gretzky was sold to the Edmonton Oilers. In Edmonton, Wayne became the most dominant player in the history of the game. Here, Wayne was playing with phenomenal hockey players. During his rookie year with the Oilers, Gretzky became the youngest player to ever score 50 goals during one season. He won the Hart Trophy as the league's MVP and tied with Marcel Dionne for the league's lead in points.

In the 1980 to 1981 season, Wayne won his first of seven scoring titles and broke Bobby Orr's assists record with 109 assists. In the same year, Wayne shattered Phil Esposito's scoring record of 76 goals by scoring 92 times. In the same year, he earned 212 points. This was the first of four times that he'd score more than 200 points and he still holds the record.

Gretzky had a style all his own. It was unique and difficult to penetrate. The area behind the opposition's goal was referred to as Gretzky's office. It was from this position that Gretzky made perfect passes for goals. He was also a great penalty killer, often scoring when his team was shorthanded.

In 1983, the Oilers went to the Stanley Cup finals and lost horribly in four straight games to the Islanders. The Oilers rebounded the next year to win the Stanley Cup and continued to for the next four years. In 1988, after the Oilers had won their fifth Stanley Cup, Gretzky gathered his teammates at center ice for an on-ice group photo which started a hockey tradition for every team at all levels and it was the last time that Wayne would wear an Oilers' sweater.

In August of the same year, it was announced that Wayne Gretzky had been traded to the Los Angeles Kings in one of the most lucrative trades in NHL history. Fans and media were not very happy as their star hockey player was heading for the United States and would never wear a Canadian team sweater again in the NHL. The Oilers were never the same, but the LA Kings were sold out every game. While playing for the Kings, Gretzky scored his 802nd goal to pass Gordie Howe's all-time leading score as well as his 1,852nd point to pass Howe as an all time point-getter in the league.

After the Kings, Wayne played for St. Louis for a short while and then signed with the New York Rangers. Although Wayne still scored well, he found the team was only mediocre and decided to retire in 1999. At the same time the NHL also retired his number 99. Not only is Wayne Gretzky considered one of the greatest players to represent the NHL, he is also one of the finest men hockey has ever known. ★

Wayne Gretzky

Name: _____ Date: _____

Reading Skills

Answer the following questions with complete sentences.

1. Does the size of a hockey player make any difference in his ability to perform well in the sport?
   _____
   _____

2. Why were so many people doubtful about Wayne's ability to play NHL hockey?
   _____
   _____

3. What hockey skills did Gretzky focus on while he was growing up?
   _____
   _____

4. During his hockey career, which team do you think provided him with the most rewards and enjoyment? Tell why.
   _____
   _____

5. What hockey tradition did Gretzky begin when he played for the Edmonton Oilers?
   _____
   _____

6. What event was the turning point in Gretzky's career and his life?
   _____
   _____

7. Why were people upset when they heard about Wayne leaving the Oilers?
   _____
   _____

8. Which famous hockey legends had their records broken by Gretzky?
   _____
   _____

9. Do you think Wayne Gretzky enjoyed his hockey career as much when he played in the United States?
   _____
   _____

Vocabulary Skills

A. The word "scrawny" begin with the blend "scr". Record the "scr" words in the box on the lines beside their meanings.

scrunch	scrimp	scrounge
scroll	scrabble	scribble
scribe	scraggly	scramble

1. to crunch or squeeze _____
2. to be very cheap _____
3. a roll of special paper _____
4. to mooch; sponge; beg _____
5. a game using letters _____
6. to write quickly _____
7. one who writes _____
8. to mix together _____
9. unkempt; shaggy _____

B. Rewrite each group of words to form a sentence about Wayne Gretzky.

1. perhaps, Wayne, Gretzky, the, most, childhood, lived, famous, athlete, any, of
   _____
   _____

2. was, when, Wayne, he, fourteen, and, decided, to, Brantford, leave, because, players, made, jealous, him, parents, unhappy, and, Toronto, Nats, play, the, for, to
   _____
   _____
   _____
   _____

3. most, was, the, Wayne's, game, versus, Union, Game, 2, memorable, Soviet, during 1987, Cup, the Canada, the
   _____
   _____
   _____
   _____

ISBN: 9781554950898   SSJ1-78 • Male Athletes

The Kid From Caroline — ★ Kurt Browning ★

Kurt Browning is one of Canada's most famous figure skating stars and is the best entertainer the sport has ever seen. His personality and rapport with the audience shines through his performances, which makes him adored and admired everywhere that he goes.

Kurt was born in Rocky Mountain House, Alberta, on June 18, 1966 and was raised in the small town of Caroline, in the foothills of the Rockies. When Kurt was three, he began to learn how to skate on a small outdoor rink made by his father. In time, Kurt began to play hockey and in order for him to have more ice time to improve his skating skills, his parents enrolled him in a figure skating class. When Kurt reached the age of 11, he had to choose between hockey and figure skating. It was an easy decision for Kurt as he liked figure skating from the beginning and knew that he was too small for hockey.

In the following years, time and talent contributed to his quick rise through the ranks of local, regional, provincial, and national events. Kurt is the only skater to place first in all three categories: novice, junior, and senior, and was Canadian National Champion four times.

In 1988, Kurt caught the world's attention at the World Figure Skating Championships in Hungary. It was here where Kurt completed a perfect quadruple toe loop, which was the first of its kind to be successfully executed in competition. He finished in sixth place and earned a place in the Guiness Book of World Records. In 1989, with a program loaded with technically difficult moves such as six triple jumps, a triple, triple combination, and his trademark quadruple toe loop, Browning's execution of his program dazzled the judges and he claimed the World title.

During the years of 1990 and 1991, Browning reclaimed his World Title and became the first Canadian, to win three consecutive world titles. In both years he was awarded the Lionel Conacher award as Canada's male athlete of the year. This was the first time that this honour had been bestowed upon a figure skater.

At the Albertville Olympics in 1992, Kurt had been plagued with a back problem, which prevented him from skating his best and reaching the podium. He did manage to place sixth. In the same year, at the World Figure Skating

Championships in California, Kurt skated well and won a silver medal.

In 1993, Kurt won the World Figure Skating Championships with his memorable program, in which he impersonated the famous character Rick Blaine, from the classic 1942 film Casablanca. Fans and the judges loved the classy, artistic, and athletic program.

The year 1994 did not turn out the way that Kurt had planned. He was the favourite going into the Lillehammer Olympics in Norway. After completing a disastrous short program, Browning found himself in 12th place. Fans and the media couldn't believe what had happened to Canada's star skater. Fortunately, Kurt rebounded with a spectacular long program and finished in 5th place.

Shortly after the Olympics, Kurt retired from amateur skating to enter the world of professional skating, where he competed in various competitions, winning three World Pro Titles. He performed in American and Canadian Stars on Ice, a show which toured North America. Kurt also delighted television audiences with various skating specials. His achievements have been honoured with his induction into Canada's Walk of Fame, the Canadian Figure Skating Hall of Fame, and the Canadian Sports Hall of Fame. ★

Kurt Browning

Name: _____ Date: _____

Reading Skills

Record, on the line provided at the end of each sentence, either the word "fact" or "opinion."

1. Kurt Browning is the greatest figure skater that Canada has ever had. _____
2. Kurt Browning was Canada's Senior Champion for four years. _____
3. Figure Skating skills improve the skating skills of hockey players. _____
4. Skaters who are small in stature make better figure skaters. _____
5. Talent, skating ability, and training made Kurt Browning a champion in figure skating. _____
6. Athletes who come from small communities usually do better in sports than those who come from large cities. _____
7. Kurt Browning's trademark jump is a quadruple toe loop. _____
8. People say Kurt retired from competitive skating due to his disastrous showing at the Olympics. _____
9. In one important competition, Kurt rebounded from 12th place to finish in 5th place with a spectacular long program. _____
10. Kurt Browning loved to perform and entertain audiences as an amateur and as a professional skater. _____
11. People consider Kurt Browning's Casablanca routine the best one that he ever performed. _____
12. Kurt Browning was an amateur and professional figure skating champion. _____

Vocabulary Skills

A. Circle the adjectives that describe Kurt Browning.

small	amusing	awkward
shy	athletic	arrogant
quick	talented	humble
wiry	obnoxious	caring
energetic	tall	hardworking
lazy	disinterested	stubborn
artistic	entertaining	boring
classy	outgoing	happy
negative	bubbly	enthusiastic

B. In some words, a pair of double consonants are found in the middle or at the end. Complete the following words with the correct pair of double letters.

(ll, tt, nn, ss, zz, ff, pp)

1. ra __ __ ort
2. enro __ __ ed
3. di __ __ icult
4. da __ __ led
5. cla __ __ y
6. profe __ __ ional
7. foothi __ __ s
8. ski __ __ s
9. begi __ __ ing
10. fo __ __ owing
11. a __ __ ention
12. technica __ __ y

C. Many words contain the following vowel combinations.

(ai, ou, oo, ee, oa)

Complete each word with its correct vowel combination.

1. entert __ __ ner
2. r __ __ sed
3. __ __ td __ __ r
4. ch __ __ se
5. l __ __ p
6. l __ __ ded
7. thr __ __
8. r __ __ ching
9. reb __ __ nded
10. t __ __ red
11. l __ __ rn
12. __ __ sy

ISBN: 9781554950898

World's Fastest Man ★ Donovan Bailey ★

Donovan Bailey is a five-time World and Olympic champion. He has been inducted into the Canada's Sports Hall of Fame twice. Once in 2004, as an individual and in 2008, as part of the 1996 Summer Olympics 4x100 relay team.

Donovan was born on December 16, 1967 in Manchester, Jamaica. He is one of five sons of George and Daisy Bailey, who believed that hard work made you a better person. As a child in Jamaica, Donovan was responsible for helping to look after the family's chickens, goats and pigs before he went to school. When Donovan was 11, his parents emigrated to Canada and lived in Oakville, Ontario in 1981.

During high school, Donovan played basketball and participated in track and field. In both sports he excelled and after graduating from high school, he could have had a career in track and field, but he wanted to prove himself in the business world and to accumulate some of the concrete things that money could buy. Education was the key to obtaining a job in order to acquire such items, so Donovan decided to attend Sheridan College in Oakville and graduated with a degree in economics. He became a self-made man and worked as a marketing and property consultant. He also ran a business in which he imported and exported clothing. At the age of 22, Donovan owned his own home and drove a Porsche convertible.

In 1991, the track lured him back to training seriously as a sprinter. At the 1995 World Track and Field Championships, Bailey won the 100 m sprint and the 4x100 m relay titles. In 1996, Bailey peaked as a sprinter during the Olympic Games in Atlanta Georgia, where he won the gold medal in the 100 m and set a world-record time of 9.84 seconds. Using his signature style of starting at the back of the pack and then using a dramatic surge in the middle of the race, Donovan overtook the other competitors and became the fastest man in history.

Donovan's win at the Olympics restored Canadians' faith in their country's athletes, whose image had been tarnished by Ben Johnson's disqualification in the 1988 Summer Olympics in Seoul, Korea, when he tested positive for steroids. Donovan did become a star in Canada, but he felt that he did not receive the attention that he envisioned. Donovan took great pride in being a "clean" athlete, but felt the media constantly compared him to Ben Johnson because of their heritage.

In 1997, Bailey won a third world title with the Canadian relay team, while he finished second in the 100 m behind Maurice Greene. In June of the same year, Bailey raced against Michael Johnson, who had been advertising that he was the world's fastest man, in a special race held at Toronto's Sky Dome. The race was to be 150 m in length. During the race, Johnson clutched his thigh in pain leaving Bailey to win the race and to claim the biggest athletic prize in history: $1.5 million dollars.

In 1998, Donovan ruptured his Achilles tendon during a basketball game with his friends and it was doubtful, even after surgery, that he would ever compete again. Fortunately Donovan did recover and was able to resume his career. In the year 2000, he was again ranked Canada's number one sprinter, but could not clinch a world title.

In 2001, Donovan Bailey announced his retirement. After racing, Donovan resumed working in the business field and began his own company called DBX Sport Management, which helps amateur athletes find a way to promote themselves. He also owns a sports injury therapy centre in Oakville. ★

Donovan Bailey

Name: _____ Date: _____

Reading Skills

In which year, did each of the following events take place in Donovan Bailey's life? Record the year on the line provided.

1. Donovan Bailey decided to take sprinting seriously. _____

2. The Bailey family moved to Canada. _____

3. Donovan injured himself seriously while having fun. _____

4. Unfortunately, Donovan could not win a world title. _____

5. Donovan won a gold medal at an Olympics competition. _____

6. At the World Track and Field championships, Donovan won gold in the 100 m sprint and the 4X100 m relay. _____

7. Maurice Green beat Donovan in the 100 m race. _____

8. Donovan raced against Michael Johnson to prove who was the fastest man. _____

9. Donovan Bailey decided to announce his retirement. _____

10. Donovan won the biggest athletic prize in sporting history. _____

11. Donovan set a world-record time of 9.84 seconds. _____

12. Donovan Bailey was born in Manchester, Jamaica. _____

Vocabulary Skills

On the line provided, record the word that matches each meaning.

> steroids   emigrate   accumulate
> consultant   tarnish   envision
> heritage   resume   ruptured
> surge

1. to rise and swell with great force _____

2. synthetic hormones that improve one's athletic ability _____

3. to disgrace oneself _____

4. to break; burst; break off _____

5. to begin again; go on _____

6. to collect little by little _____

7. a person who gives professional advice _____

8. to leave one's country to settle in another _____

9. to form a mental picture _____

10. trait; beliefs; customs _____

Research Skills

Using the Internet or the Resource Centre find out the answers to the following questions.

1. What are cortico steroids?

2. How do cortico steroids help people?

3. What are anabolic steroids?

4. What do anabolic steroids do to the body?

5. Why do athletes use anabolic steroids?

6. How do you feel about the usage of anabolic steriods by athletes?

Canada's King of the Hoops ★ Steve Nash ★

No one ever imagined that a skinny Canadian kid would ever become a famous NBA player, but Steve Nash proved them wrong. He refused to give up on his hoops dream and begged college coaches to take a look at him. Now, he has the basketball world at his feet.

Steve was born in Johannesburg, South Africa, on February 7, 1964. His father played professional soccer, which took the family all over the world. When his father retired from soccer, the family moved to Canada to live in Regina, and then moved to Victoria B.C. Steve was an avid athlete and excelled in a variety of sports, although his physical appearance was not athletic-looking. He loved to analyze and process information, which helped him to play games of strategy.

Steve also developed into a talented soccer player, which did not surprise people. He showed real promise on the pitch, had great speed, and a wonderful feel for the game. Unfortunately, Steve found it difficult to limit himself to one sport as he liked so many and was crazy about hockey. His favourite hockey player was Wayne Gretzky, with whom Steve could identify. Both athletes were undersized, under-estimated, and used their instincts and worked hard to show their great abilities in their chosen sport.

While in high school, Steve discovered his favourite sport - basketball - and developed a strong desire to become an NBA player. This seemed highly unlikely as Steve was slight in stature and basketball was not considered a career sport in Canada. Even though the odds were against him, Steve never gave up on his dream. He constantly worked on his skills and was quick and fearless while shooting for the basket.

Steve and his coach believed he could play major college basketball in the United States, but no one else did. His coach wrote many letters to American colleges but the response was the same: "No Thanks." Finally, a tiny Jesuit university called Santa Clara, outside of San Francisco, showed interest.

The head coach flew to Canada to watch Steve play and offered him a full scholarship. He also told Steve that he was the worst defender that he had ever seen and he would have to work at being a more complete player. Steve was very willing to do anything to fulfill his dream.

Throughout university, Steve played for the Santa Clara Broncos, steadily improving his

game and skills. His strong work ethics rubbed off on his teammates and the Broncos had a strong comeback, winning many games and championships. During his senior year, Steve began to attract the attention of the media and professional scouts at the national level. Many felt that Steve was the college game's most polished player, but the NBA scouts were still concerned about his spindly frame and his ordinary 31 inch vertical. During the draft, Steve was picked in the first round by the Phoenix Suns. He was the first Canadian to be selected so high up in the draft.

In 1998, Nash was traded to the Dallas Mavericks. For several years, Steve improved his average points per game and his ability to score. During the 2003 - 2004 season, his average points were in decline, he had been plagued with injuries, and his contract had expired. Even though Dallas still wanted him, he was offered more money and a better deal with his former team, the Phoenix Suns. During his tenure with the Suns, Nash has lead the team to improve their technique, and they have celebrated many victories and championships. Nash has also been awarded the coveted MVP award on several occasions.

Steve is also involved in many charities and has established organizations that foster health in kids affected by poverty, illness, abuse or neglect. He also sponsors a Youth Basketball League in B.C. In 2007, Steve received the Order of Canada and in 2008, he received a star on Canada's Walk of Fame. There is an old adage that applies to Steve Nash that says "One should never judge a book by its cover." ★

Steve Nash

Name: _____ Date: _____

Reading Skills

A. Complete each sentence with the correct word.

before, after, during, while

1. Steve Nash played soccer _____ he played basketball.
2. The Nash family moved to Canada _____ Steve's father retired from soccer.
3. Steve discovered the game of basketball _____ his high school years.
4. Steve's game steadily improved _____ he played for the Santa Clara Broncos.
5. _____ his senior year, many national scouts were interested in his playing ability.
6. _____ Steve was in high school, his coach wrote letters to many American colleges.
7. Santa Clara's coach told Steve he was the worst defender that he had ever seen _____ he offered him a scholarship.
8. Steve left the Dallas Mavericks _____ his contract expired.
9. _____ his father played professional soccer, the Nash family travelled all over the world.
10. _____ the draft, Steve was picked in the first round.

B. Underline words and phrases that describe Steve Nash.

passionate, tall and skinny, committed, fickle, strong work ethics, awkward, thinker, undersized, short, dedicated, lazy, fearless, polished player, greedy, team player, overweight, short, weak

Vocabulary Skills

A. Match each word in the box to its synonym.

adage	constantly	coveted
fearless	spindly	plagued
avid	foster	analyze
illness	stature	occasions

1. saying _____
2. sickness _____
3. desired _____
4. brave _____
5. times _____
6. solve _____
7. promote _____
8. height _____
9. bothered _____
10. always _____
11. enthusiastic _____
12. skinny _____

B. Use each group of words in a sentence pertaining to Steve Nash.

1. basketball, guard, Phoenix Suns
   _____
   _____
2. MVP, won, coveted
   _____
   _____
3. spindly, excelled, athlete
   _____
   _____
4. identified, compared, himself
   _____
   _____
5. media, scouts, attracted
   _____
   _____

The Greatest Blueliner ★ Bobby Orr ★

*B*obby Orr is a truly special athlete that many claim changed the game of hockey to the way it is played today. He is a quiet, humble man who is a legend in his own right. Bobby played the game his way and no other hockey player has dominated the ice, excited the fans, nor has succeeded the way he did in such a brief career.

Robert Gordon "Bobby" Orr was born in a small northern community called Parry Sound on March 20, 1948. At the age of four, Bobby learned how to skate on the Sequin River under his father's watchful eye. When he was five, he played hockey with a local league against boys two or three years older than him. While playing at the Peewee level his coach moved his hockey position from forward to defence. This move, in time, resulted in him developing his aggressive style of acceleration, fluid skating ability, and end to end rushing.

During a Bantam tournament in 1960, NHL scouts recognized his dominance on the ice and his aggressive style of playing and began pursuing him at the age of 12. When he was 14, Orr's parents allowed him to choose on his own to sign with the Boston Bruins organization. Bobby felt the Bruins were the team of the future and he wanted to be a part of their building program. That fall, Bobby was assigned to the Oshawa Generals, a junior league, and at the age of 14, Bobby was competing against 18, 19, and 20 year old players. According to NHL rules, he could not join the Boston Bruins until he was 18. His time with the Oshawa Generals allowed his body to mature and develop. In his first year, Bobby stood 5' 6" and weighed 135 pounds and by the time his junior career was over, he was a sturdy 6' and almost 200 pounds. In 1966, a prominent Toronto Lawyer negotiated his first contract with the Bruins, which made Orr the highest paid player in league history.

During his first professional game against the Detroit Red Wings, 18 year old Orr impressed the home crowd and the sports media with his defensive style of play. He performed well, blocking shots, checking, moving players away from the net, and assisting a goal. His first season with the Bruins was outstanding and won him the Calder Trophy as the best rookie. He was second in the league in scoring by a defenceman. Orr played a very physical style of hockey and some felt he was too daring during his rushes. His body was not prepared yet for the abuse it would receive.

In his first season during a daring rush, he injured his left knee. This began his long battle with knee injuries that plagued him throughout his career and caused his early retirement.

In 1970, Orr won his first Stanley Cup with a dramatic moment that was photographed and published in magazines and newspapers around the world. While scoring one of his famous goals in hockey, Orr was tripped by a Blues defenceman. In the photo, Orr is pictured flying through the air with his arms raised in victory. This prize-winning photo is probably the most famous and recognized hockey image of all time.

In 1971, Orr signed a contract with the Bruins that would pay him $1 million dollars over five years. This was the largest deal ever in hockey, orchestrated by his agent and lawyer, Alan Eagleson. While playing with the Bruins, Orr's knee continually interrupted his playing. In 1976, when the Bruins offered him an even better deal, his lawyer falsely told him that the Chicago Black Hawks had a better deal. Orr did sign with Chicago, but his injuries were so painful that it was impossible for him to play. Orr decided to retire at the age of 30 after 657 games and 917 points.

Although Orr's career was shorter than most hockey players, he did acquire fame and success. He won the Norris Trophy for eight consecutive seasons and won the Hart Trophy three times. He revolutionized hockey with his outstanding scoring ability, playmaking from the blue line, his rapid acceleration, and his control and dominance in a game. He is truly a great athlete and ambassador of hockey. ★

Bobby Orr

Name: _____ Date: _____

Reading Skills

Complete each activity carefully using sentence answers.

1. What influenced the development of Bobby Orr's style of playing hockey when he was young?
   _____
   _____

2. Why were NHL scouts interested in Orr at the Bantam tournament?
   _____
   _____

3. Describe Bobby Orr's playing style.
   _____
   _____
   _____

4. How did Bobby Orr's playing affect spectators?
   _____
   _____

5. When did Orr begin to experience problems with his knee?
   _____
   _____

6. Why were some people concerned with Orr's physical style of hockey?
   _____
   _____

7. Describe the dramatic moment that took place in Orr's career in 1970?
   _____
   _____
   _____

8. Describe the ways in which Orr revolutionized hockey.
   _____
   _____

Vocabulary Skills

A. Match each word in the box to its meaning. Record it on the line provided.

dominate	aggressive	acceleration
prominent	fluid	revolutionize
ambassador	defensive	orchestrated

1. _____: ready to protect or defend
2. _____: speeding up; increasing
3. _____: to control or rule by strength
4. _____: flowing smoothly
5. _____: very active; energetic
6. _____: well known; important
7. _____: arranged; composed
8. _____: to produce a very great change
9. _____: a person of good will

B. Classify each pair of words as antonyms or synonyms by recording A or S on the line provided.

1. brief   short   ____
2. ability   talent   ____
3. manner   style   ____
4. diasppointed   impressed   ____
5. amateur   professional   ____
6. contract   agreement   ____
7. stopped   interrupted   ____
8. future   present   ____

C. Record the number of syllables heard in each of the following words on the line provided.

1. dominance   ____   5. orchestrated ____
2. acceleration ____   6. organization ____
3. consecutive   ____   7. league   ____
4. aggressive   ____   8. media   ____

The Pugilist Specialist ★ Lennox Lewis ★

Lennox Lewis is a retired heavyweight boxer who competed as an amateur for Canada and a professional for Britain. In his prime, he stood 1.96 m (6' 5") tall, weighed 113 kg (250 lb) and had an exceptional reach that measured 210 cm (84 in). He is one of three boxers in history, along with Muhammad Ali and Evander Holyfield, to have won the heavyweight championship three times.

Lennox was born in West Ham, London, England, in 1965, to parents with Jamaican heritage. In 1977, when Lennox was 12, his mother decided to take him and his brother to live in Canada. They resided in Kitchener, Ontario, where Lennox attended high school. At school, classmates teased him about his accent which made him very angry and he became involved in many fights. After being punished three times for fighting, a teacher advised him to take his frustrations and anger out in sports. Lennox took up boxing as it was a one on one sport which he liked. In 1978, he had his first amateur match and by the early 1980s, Lennox was becoming recognized as an impressive boxer.

In 1983, at the Canada Winter Games and the World Junior Championships, Lennox won gold medals. That year he was named athlete of the year in Canada. During the years from 1984 to 1987, Lennox won gold medals at the National Senior Championships, the Commonwealth Games, and the Pan Am games. From 1984 to 1988, he was the Canadian Heavyweight Champion every year. In 1984, Lennox represented Canada in the Los Angeles Olympics as a Super Heavyweight. He made it out of the quarter finals, but lost a controversial decision to the American boxer Tyrell Biggs and had to settle for a fifth place finish.

His loss at the Olympics was a heart-breaking defeat, but Lennox decided to stay amateur for another four years so he could have another crack at the gold medal. In 1988, at the Seoul Summer Olympics in Korea, Lennox was anxious to achieve his goal. He was determined to win this time and defeated his first opponent with a second-round TKO. His next adversary was knocked out in the first round. His third opponent withdrew which meant Lennox would go to the final bout against American Riddick Bowe, who had less than three rounds of fighting under his belt. During this gold medal match, Lennox defeated Bowe with a technical knockout in the second round. Lennox's victory ended a 56 year drought for Canada's Olympic boxers. He became the first Canadian to win an Olympic boxing gold medal since Toronto's Horace "Lefty" Gwynne was crowned bantamweight champion at the 1932 Amsterdam Games.

After the Olympics, Lennox turned professional and returned to England as he had always considered himself more British than Canadian. Unfortunately fans felt his decision to return was more for monetary reasons than homesickness for England. His professional career rose quickly in the world rankings. In 1990, he captured the European heavyweight title. In March of 1991, he added the British heavyweight title and the Commonwealth title in April of 1992. By this time, Lennox was one of the top five heavyweights in the world. Lennox was truly talented. He was a great boxer and great puncher. His right hand delivered his knockout punch as well as a strong jab.

During his career, Lennox had 44 professional fights with a record of 41 wins with 32 knockouts, two losses, and a draw. He has fought famous fighters such as Mike Tyson, Evander Holyfield, and Donovan "Razor" Ruddock victoriously. In June of 2003, shortly after his last fight at a press conference, Lennox announced that he would be retiring from boxing. He became the third boxer to join two other boxing greats - Rocky Marciano and Gene Tunney - to retire as world heavyweight champion. He had been best in the world as a junior, an Olympic Champion, and world heavyweight champion. He had done it all and there was nothing left to fight for. ★

Lennox Lewis

Name: _____   Date: _____

Reading Skills

Sentences often provide a great deal of information. Read each sentence carefully. Decide if each sentence tells you the following:

who, what, why, when, where, how, how many

There may be more than one answer.

1. Lennox Lewis won the heavyweight championship three times.
   _____

2. Lennox was teased at school by classmates for the way he talked.
   _____

3. In 1988, at the Seoul Olympics in Korea, Lennox was determined to win a gold medal.
   _____

4. During the gold medal match, Lennox defeated his opponent with a technical knockout in the second round.
   _____

5. Feelings of disappointment crept over Lennox when he lost to Tyrell Biggs at the 1984 Olympics.
   _____

6. Lennox knocked out his second opponent in the first round with a hard punch to the jaw.
   _____

7. Lennox had 44 professional fights with a record of 41 wins with 32 knockouts, two losses and a draw.
   _____

8. Lennox returned to England when he turned professional because he was homesick for his first home.
   _____

9. Lennox Lewis was 1.96 m tall and weighed 113 kg.
   _____

Vocabulary Skills

Develop your pugilistic word skills! Match each word in the box to its meaning.

```
glass jaw            bout      palooka
saved by the bell    clinch    combination
to take a dive       jab       south paw
down for the count   hook      sucker punch
breadbasket          gate      draw
```

1. a boxing match consisting of rounds with one minute breaks _____

2. a boxer who is easily knocked out _____

3. a poor boxer with no ability _____

4. One boxer holds onto the other to avoid being hit. _____

5. boxer pretends to be knocked out _____

6. a series of punches thrown in sequence _____

7. A boxer is knocked down for the count to ten. _____

8. an inside punch _____

9. left-handed fighter _____

10. the bell signals the end of the round before the referee finished the count _____

11. Both boxers tie or earn equal number of points during a fight. _____

12. a punch thrown quickly and the most often _____

13. the stomach area _____

14. an unexpected punch _____

15. The total amount of money that a boxing match brings in. _____

Canada's Swimming Pool Wonder ★ Alex Baumann ★

Alex Baumann is one of Canada's outstanding athletes in the pool. As he headed for the 1984 Olympic Games in Los Angeles, his and Canada's hopes were high. Two tragic events took place in Alex's life prior to this important event. His father died from diabetes and his depressed brother committed suicide. Fortunately, Alex had the inner strength to deal with his family loss and the pressure of competing. He also knew that Canadians were pulling for him. Like all the great Canadian Olympians who have preceded him, Baumann produced under pressure and earned two gold medals. His medals were the first in swimming for Canada since 1912.

Alexander ("Alex") Sasha Baumann was born April 21, 1964 in Prague, the Czech Republic. His family left Prague in 1967 when his father secured a temporary position at Christchurch University in New Zealand. When the family was supposed to return to their homeland, the Soviets had invaded their country. The Baumanns decided to move to Sudbury, Ontario, Canada in late 1969 when Alex's father was hired by Laurentian University.

Alex became involved with swimming at the age of nine, and was a natural in the pool. He soon began competitive swimming and trained at the Laurentian University under Jeno Tihanyi, who was the first to integrate sports science into the art of coaching. During Alex's first official swim race, he failed to touch the wall with both hands and was disqualified in the 50 m breaststroke. It was a very upsetting moment for him, but a good lesson to learn early. Alex went back to the pool and trained even harder and in his next race, he finished third. Within a year, he was breaking national records in his age category.

By the age of 17, Alex had made 38 Canadian swimming records and held the world record in the 200 m individual medley and quickly became one of Canada's favourites. He accepted a swimming scholarship at Indiana University and began swimming on the university swim team. While training, he developed chronic pain in his shoulder and returned to Sudbury to receive physical therapy and training under his former coach. This injury caused him to sit out the 1982 World Aquatic Championships in Ecuador, but it had improved enough that he was able to win gold in both the 200 and 400 m individual medley events at the 1982 Commonwealth Games in Brisbane, Australia. In 1983, Alex won the 400 m individual medley event at the World University Games.

Alex was on a high and was well ready for the Olympic Games when tragedy struck with the death of his father, which devastated him. Alex retreated to the water for therapy. At the 1984 Olympics, Alex was selected to carry the Canadian flag at the Los Angeles Olympics opening ceremonies which he did just as proudly as he had at the 1982 Commonwealth Games and the 1983 University Games.

Although Baumann was known for his youthful cool and cerebral confidence, he did find he couldn't sleep prior to his first event. All he could think of was his expectations and those of a medal-hungry nation. Still feeling tense after several heats, he decided to do something that he had never done before. He went and had a rub down to get rid of the tension so he would be relaxed.

On July 30, Alex swam an outstanding 400 m individual medley in four minutes, 17.41 seconds breaking his own world record by over a tenth of a second. His gold medal in this event was the first one for Canada in 71 years. Five days later, in record time, Alex captured the 200 m individual medley. During the Olympic Games, Alex Baumann and Victor Davis had incredible success for Canada winning five medals (three gold and five silver). Alex was named Male Athlete of the Year, inducted into the Olympic Hall of Fame in 1985, and joined the Canadian Sports Hall of Fame in 1987. In 1984, he received the Order of Canada. ★

Alex Baumann

Name: _____ Date: _____

Reading Skills

Circle the correct answer(s) to each question.

1. In which of the following countries had the Baumann family lived.
   England   United States   Czech Republic
   Australia   Equador   New Zealand

2. In how many competitions has Alex been the Canadian flag bearer?
   five   four   one   three   ten

3. In which city did the Baumans choose to make their final home?
   Christchurch   Los Angeles   London
   Prague   Sudbury   Sarnia

4. How many Canadian swimming records had Alex made by the age of 17?
   28   45   23   108   38   58

5. What medals did Alex win at the 1982 Commonwealth Games?
   2 silver   1 gold   1 bronze   2 gold   3 silver

6. What feelings did Alex experience prior to his first major event at the Olympics.
   confidant   nervous   loose   tense   scared

7. Which state university offered Alex a swimming scholarship?
   Utah   Idaho   Indiana   New York   Illinois

8. In which month of the year does Alex celebrate his birthday?
   August   April   March   June   September

9. How many years had past since a Canadian swimmer had won a gold medal?
   63   89   72   41   35   100

10. In which year had the last Canadian won an Olympic swimming medal?
    1972   1918   1937   1912   2000

Vocabulary Skills

A. Match each word in the box to its meaning. Record each word on the line provided.

> preceded   category   tragedy
> temporary   medley   cerebral
> integrate   chronic   tension

1. _____: mental strain; nervous anxiety
2. _____: appealing to the intellect
3. _____: an intensely sad event
4. _____: prolonged; lingering
5. _____: jumble; mix
6. _____: a class or division
7. _____: unify; bring together
8. _____: used for a short time only
9. _____: to go before

B. Explain the following terms in your own words.

1. "natural in the pool" _____
2. "pulling" for him" _____
3. "to sit out" _____
4. "on a high" _____
5. "medal hungry" _____
6. "cerebral confidence" _____

C. Use one of the terms in a good sentence.
_____
_____

Woman of the Games 2006 ★ Cindy Klassen ★

Cindy Klassen is a Canadian speed skater and Canada's most decorated Olympian. At the age of two, Cindy was introduced to hockey by her father. When she was five, she began playing hockey and soccer with local clubs. During high school, Cindy was an avid athlete who tried to squeeze in as many sports as she could. Although she had a wide variety of interests, her main focus was hockey.

Cindy played boys' hockey during most of her life and reached the double and triple A levels in her home province of Alberta. She thrived on the intense training that she received from the hockey coaches. Her goal was to play on the women's hockey team for Canada at the Olympics in 1998. During 1995, Cindy played on Manitoba's female hockey team and when she reached the age of 16, she switched to Senior Women's hockey and was chosen to play on the Junior National Team at Lake Placid in the United States in 1996. Things were moving along as she hoped until 1997, when she was not selected for the 1998 Olympic Women's Hockey Team.

With her Olympic dream destroyed Cindy was devastated and depressed. What was she to do now as she did not have an alternate plan? Her parents encouraged her to take up speed skating since her skating skills were so strong. Her immediate reaction was not a positive one. When Cindy was younger, she and some of her hockey friends had made fun of the long blades and skin tight outfits of speed skaters. After giving her parents' suggestion some thought, Cindy decided to give speed skating a try. Off she went to the Susan Auch Oval thinking speed skating would be a breeze. Much to her surprise, Cindy found it was harder to do than it looked but with the encouragement of the various coaches, Cindy rapidly improved.

In a year, Cindy was on the roster for the Manitoba long-track team that was to compete at the Canada Winter Games in 1999, in Cornerbrook, Newfoundland. Unfortunately, the ice melted and the long-track events never took place. Cindy did compete at various Canada Cup events and earned a spot on the Junior National Team in February of 1999. At this competition, she won the 1000 meter race and took third place in the 500 meter race.

In the year 2000, Cindy made the National Team and in 2001, she earned three top 10 finishes at the World Single Distance Championships, including a bronze in the 1500 meter race. In 2002, Cindy collected a bronze medal in the 3000 meter race as well as fourth place finishes in the 1500 meter and the 5000 meter races.

Cindy was flying high and on her way until one day during training, she experienced a dreadful mishap. While rounding a corner, Cindy crashed into a group of skaters. Her right arm was cut from her wrist to the elbow by a skater's blade. It sliced through 12 tendons, a nerve, and a major artery. Everyone felt that Cindy's skating season was over but two months later, she was training again with a splint on her arm. Cindy's 2004 to 2005 season was very successful. She won the World Cup title in the 1500 meter as well as first place in the 1500 meter and 3000 meter at the World Single Distance Championships.

At the 2006 Winter Olympics in Torino, Italy, Cindy won a bronze medal in the 3000 meter, a silver in the 1000 meter as well as a team silver in the Pursuit. She struck gold in the 1500 meter race which was her specialty. In her most dreaded race the 5000 meter she won a bronze.

Cindy Klassen will go down in the Canadian sporting records as the first Canadian Olympian to win five medals in one Olympic Games and the only Canadian with six Olympic medals. ★

Cindy Klassen

Name: _____ Date: _____

Reading Skills

Locate a sentence in the biography that proves each of the following statements about Cindy Klassen are true. Record the first six words of the sentence on the line provided.

1. Cindy Klassen had a goal in mind while she played boys' hockey.
   _____

2. Cindy found out that long range plans don't always come true.
   _____

3. Cindy's parents were supportive and tried to help her?
   _____

4. Cindy's negative response to her parents' suggestion was for a reason.
   _____

5. Speed skating is a difficult sport.
   _____

6. Cindy's strong skating skills and her eagerness to work helped her speed skating to move quickly.
   _____

7. An unfortunate accident almost ended Cindy's speed skating career.
   _____

8. Cindy Klassen is a determined and feisty athlete.
   _____

9. Cindy Klassen is Canada's most decorated Olympic athlete.
   _____

Vocabulary Skills

A. Use the following pairs of antonyms to complete each sentence.

most - least	happy - depressed
strong - weak	easy - difficult
positive - negative	

1. Cindy's reaction to her parents' suggestion went from _____ to _____.

2. Although speedskating looked _____ to do, Cindy found it _____ at first.

3. Cindy was _____ with her hockey career's direction but became _____ when she didn't make the Olympic Women's Team.

4. Cindy's skating skills were _____ but her speedskating style was _____ at first.

5. She won gold in her _____ favourite race and bronze in her _____ favourite race.

B. Underline the words that best describe Cindy Klassen's personality.

energetic	lazy	loses interest
avid athlete	courageous	fearless
weak	able to focus	positive
insecure	disinterested	fickle
goal oriented	successful	hardworking
thinker	fighter	

Research Skills

Using the Internet or the resource centre, research to find out the answers to the following questions.

1. What is speedskating?

2. What are the different types of speedskating?

A Whiz on Wheels ★ Chantal Petitclerc ★

Chantal Petitclerc is a Canadian wheelchair racer and has had a very successful career in this sport. She was born on December 15, 1969 in Saint-Marc-des-Carrières in Quebec. At the age of 13, while playing with some friends on a farm near her home town, a heavy barn door fell on her. She was paralyzed from the waist down and lost the use of her legs. During an interview, Chantal stated that she always accepted her accident but the first year of her recovery was the hardest. While attending high school, her physical education teacher convinced her to take up swimming to develop her physical strength and stamina. This was Chantal's introduction to sports and to training.

While attending Laval University in Quebec City, she was introduced to wheelchair sports by trainer Pierre Pomerleau. Chantal took part in her first race, using a homemade wheelchair and came dead last trailing way behind the other competitors. It was then that Chantal fell in love with this sport and thus began the dazzling climb of this Canadian athlete as a specialist in wheelchair racing.

At 18, Chantal participated in her first formal wheelchair race in Sherbrooke, Quebec and returned with the title "Most Promising" and a real racing wheelchair. Chantal competed in many Canadian competitions, proving that she had the talent and the determination to reach the podium.

While developing her skills as a wheelchair athlete, Chantal pursued her studies in social science at the Sainte-Foy College and then studied history at the University of Alberta where she was able to train with Peter Eriksson, a former world class speedskater, who became her coach.

In 1992, Chantal participated in the Paralympic Games for the first time in Barcelona, Spain. She returned with two bronze medals that began her collection of 21 Paralympic medals. Chantal has also participated in competitions of all distances such as sprints, middle-distance races, and marathons. In the T4 class, Chantal holds the Canadian record in all the events and the record in the world 100 meter race. At the Atlanta Paralympic Games in the United States in 1996, Chantal won gold medals in the 100 and 200 meter events

and three silver medals in the 400, 800, and 1400 meter races. As well as individual races, Chantal has won wheelchair marathons in many cities across Canada.

At the Sydney Paralympics in Australia, Chantal won two gold and two silver medals in wheelchair racing. Her most remarkable exploit was at the Olympic and Paralympic Games in Athens, Greece in 2004, when she won five Paralympic gold medals and a first place in the 800 meter race in the Olympics, which was a demonstration sport.

The Summer Paralympics in Beijing, China, in 2008, was to be Chantal's last competitive games. Her glorious career came to a close with five gold medals. Chantal Petitclerc's determination, perseverance, and success has made her a super role model for all Canadians, those with and those without disablilities. Hopefully, Chantal's dream of the day, the International Olympic Committee granting wheelchair racing official Olympic status, will come true in the near future. ★

Chantal Petitclerc

Name: _____ Date: _____

Reading Skills

Complete each sentence with the correct words from the biography.

1. Chantal Petitclerc was _____ at the age of 13 when a heavy _____ _____ fell on her.

2. Chantal took up _____ to improve her _____ and _____.

3. During one of her earlier races, Chantal used a _____ _____.

4. Chantal raced in _____, middle-distance races and _____.

5. In her first Paralympics in _____, Spain, Chantal won _____ _____ medals.

6. At the Atlantic _____ Games in the _____ in 1996, Chantal won two _____ medals and three _____ medals.

7. At the _____ Paralympics, Chantal won _____ gold medals and two _____ medals in wheelchair racing.

8. During the Paralympics Games in _____, Greece and _____, China, Chantal came home with ten _____ medals.

9. While training to become a wheelchair _____, Chantal studied _____ science and _____ at university.

10. Chantal Petitclerc is a fantastic _____ _____ for all Canadians.

Vocabulary Skills

A. In each of the following words, circle the prefix, underline the root word, or box the suffix.

1. remarkable
2. hardest
3. trailing
4. international
5. swimming
6. recovery
7. specialist
8. successful

B. Divide each of the following words into syllables on the line provided.

1. paralyzed _____
2. interview _____
3. competitor _____
4. determination _____
5. individual _____
6. marathons _____

C. Record each group of words in the correct alphabetical order on the line provided.

1. wheelchair, won, waist, world, where
   _____

2. friends, farm, former, future, first
   _____

3. status, stamina, sports, strength, specialist
   _____

4. middle, many, marathons, meter, medals
   _____

5. competed, coach, competitors, career, collection
   _____

Canada's Champion Hurdler ★ Perdita Felicien ★

Hurdling is a kind of track and field race. The athlete runs and strides over a structure called a hurdle. Peridita Felicien is a Canadian track and field hurdler. She was born in Oshawa, Ontario on August 29, 1980 and raised in Pickering Ontario.

Perdita began competing in track and field events and started with the 100 meter dash as she was inspired by World and Olympic champions Donovan Bailey and Bruni Surin from Canada. During her high school years at Pineridge Secondary School in Pickering, Perdita dedicated herself to hurdling and won the Ontario High School Hurdling Championship in 1997. This feat earned her the Athlete of the Year award at Pineridge.

In 1998, Perdita was the Ontario High School Champion again and also added the first of two consecutive Canadian Junior Championships. At a scholastic meet in Ohio, her performance brought her offers of athletic scholarships from several American universities. Perdita chose to attend the University of Illinois, where she enrolled in the study of Kinesiology.

During her first year of competing at the university level, Perdita earned All-American honours and set the record for the fastest time by a freshman in NCAA history in the 100 meter hurdles. In the next year, Perdita was ranked number one in the 100 meter hurdles by the NCAA for the entire outdoor season. She became the first Illinois athlete to ever win an indoor and outdoor season national championships. Perdita was the Illinois Female Athlete of the Year for three consecutive years. She was also voted as the National Female Outdoor Athlete of the Year by the U.S. Track Coaches Association.

During 2003, Perdita won her second consecutive 100 meter hurdle national title. She was named the Big Ten Conference "Athlete of the Year" which was a first for a University of Illinois female athlete. In the same year, she was honoured with the title NCAA Female Track and Field Athlete of the Year.

With all these accolades and honours, Perdita became a major force on the international scene for hurdling. In 2003, at the World Championships in Paris, France, Perdita won the 100 meter hurdles final. With this win, she became Canada's first ever female gold medallist and the first female in Illinois

track and field history to win a gold medal in an individual event at the World Championships. Perdita was named Canada's Female Athlete of the Year and was the first track athlete in 25 years to capture this honour.

In March of 2004, Perdita had to go up against the hurdling great Gail Divers at the IAAF World Championships in Budapest, Hungary. She not only beat Gail Divers, but set a new record. After this competition, Perdita won six more hurdling events that lead up to the Summer Olympics in Athens, Greece in 2004.

In the Athens Olympics, Perdita was expected to win gold in the 100 meter hurdles. On August 23, 2004, an unfortunate event took place. Perdita failed to clear the first hurdle and fell into the adjacent lane knocking down the Russian athlete and taking her out of the race as well. Perdita was shocked and devastated after the accident, not only for herself, but for the other athlete as well.

Perdita did return to the track and has had some success winning medals at various events. In 2007, she won a silver medal at the World Championships in the hurdles. In 2008, Perdita did not have the chance to redeem her self-esteem and her reputation in the hurdles at the Olympics in Beijing, as she had to withdraw due to a foot injury. ★

Perdita Felicien

Name: _____ Date: _____

Reading Skills

Answer each question with a complete sentence.

1. Where and when did Perdita begin competing as a hurdler?
   _____
   _____

2. What success did Perdita achieve during her high school years?
   _____
   _____

3. What other Canadian Championship did she win two years in a row?
   _____
   _____

4. What did her athletic performance bring when she competed in Ohio?
   _____
   _____

5. Which university did Perdita choose and what did she study?
   _____
   _____

6. What is Kinesiology and why do you think she chose it to study?
   _____
   _____

7. Why was Perdita named Canada's Female Athlete of the Year in 2003?
   _____
   _____

8. Why did Perdita not complete her race in the Athens Olympics?
   _____
   _____

9. If Perdita had been able to compete at the Beijing Olympics, what thoughts might have crossed her mind before the race?
   _____
   _____

Vocabulary Skills

A *hurdle* is the structure which a *hurdler* strides over. In the words *hurdle* and *hurdler,* the letters "ur" make the "r" sound. Complete the crossword puzzle with words that have the "ur" sound and match each meaning.

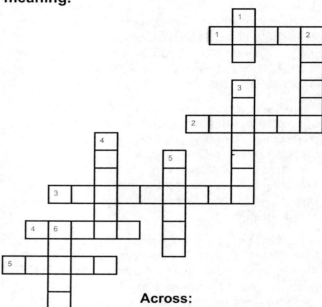

Across:
1. an explosion
2. a dark, rich colour
3. meat in a bun
4. worn by a cowboy
5. works in a hospital

Down:
1. an animal's coat
2. an animal with a shell
3. a thief
4. to talk softly
5. a farm bird
6. used to carry money

Research Skills

Using the Internet or the resource centre, research the sport of hurdling. Find out the skills an athlete would need in order to participate in the sport.

ISBN: 9781554950898   24   SSJ1-78 • Female Athletes

Canada's Skiing Trailblazer ★ Beckie Scott ★

Beckie Scott is an elite cross-country skier who blazed a trail for fellow Canadian skiers on a brilliant mid-winter day in 2002 at Soldier Hollow, Utah, capturing the bronze medal in the pursuit race at the Salt Lake City Olympics.

Beckie was born on August 1, 1974, in Vegreville, Alberta, and grew up in Vermilion, a small Albertan community. She began cross-country skiing at the age of five. Beckie was an active child and also participated in activities such as dancing, piano, gymnastics, and swimming. Her first competitive sport was swimming but eventually skiing became her primary interest. At the age of seven, she participated in her first cross-country skiing competition.

When Beckie was 13, a new cross-country skiing coach, Len Parsons, moved to Vermilion and she began to take up skiing seriously. Parsons taught her to think big and to believe in herself. In 1988, on her first trip to the Junior National Championships, Beckie realized she had potential and enjoyed the taste of high level competition. It was then that her Olympic dream began to take shape.

The way to the top was not easy, but long and gradual, and some people wondered if her goals and dreams were realistic. Beckie believed in herself and was determined to succeed.

In 1998, at her first Olympic Games in Nagano, Japan, Beckie's best placing was 45th. In 2002, at the Salt Lake City Olympic Games, in Utah, Beckie met with great success. At Soldier Hollow, Utah, the site of the cross-country skiing events, Beckie won a bronze medal in the pursuit race. She became the first Canadian and North American woman to stand on the Olympic podium in cross-country skiing.

Beckie's moment of glory did not end on that day. Two women skiers, who had finished before her, had tested positive for performance enhancing drugs in other races. Beckie believed strongly in honesty and fair play and along with the Canadian Olympic Committee, fought to have both skiers disqualified.

In June of 2003, Beckie was presented with the silver medal that had been taken away from one of the skiers. Months later, the second skier was disqualified and Becky received the gold medal, two and a half years after the Salt Lake City Olympics. Her lengthy battle, due to her strong convictions and belief in fair play, made her a legend in the sporting world.

At the Olympics in Torino, Italy, in February 2006, Beckie and her teammate Sara Renner won a silver medal in the team sprint. During her competitive years, Beckie also captured 15 World Cup medals.

In recognition of her efforts in cross-country skiing, Beckie has been given a variety of awards in Canada and has been inducted into the Alberta Sports Hall of Fame and Canada's Hall of Fame. Beckie is a strong advocate of athletes performing drug free and helped to circulate an athletes' petition requesting the establishment of an independent drug-testing body for all World Cup and Olympic Competitions. She is also known for her support of various charities and was named a UNICEF Canada representative. At one World Cup, she challenged her fellow athletes to donate their winnings to an Afganistan relief project.

Beckie is now happily married and living in Bend, Oregon. She spends her leisure time reading, writing, and cooking. Now she puts on her cross-country skis for fun. ★

Beckie Scott

Name: _____ Date: _____

Reading Skills

Tell when each of the following events took place in Beckie Scott's life and career.

1. Beckie began to take cross-country skiing seriously.
   _____

2. Sara Renner and Beckie Scott won the silver medal in the team sprint.
   _____

3. Beckie Scott began skiing.
   _____

4. In the pursuit race, Beckie Scott won a bronze medal.
   _____

5. Becky found out she really enjoyed competing.
   _____

6. Beckie's best placing in a race was 45th.
   _____

7. Becky was given the gold medal that she had fought for and deserved.
   _____

8. Beckie Scott was the first Canadian woman cross-country skier to stand on an Olympic podium.
   _____

9. The silver medal was presented to Beckie.
   _____

10. Beckie Scott participated in her first skiing competition.
    _____

Vocabulary Skills

A. Read each clue below. Unscramble the bold letters beside it to find the word that matches the clue and record it on the line provided.

1. a synonym for bright   **allibirtn** _____
2. an antonym for lazy   **eitvca** _____
3. a synonym for skills   **otpneltia** _____
4. an antonym for fail   **decsuce** _____
5. a homonym for fare   **rfia** _____
6. an antonym for negative **tepoivsi** _____
7. a synonym for give   **teadno** _____
8. a homonym for made   **diam** _____

B. Explain the meaning of each group of words in your own words on the lines provided.

1. blazed a trail _____
   _____

2. capturing the bronze medal _____
   _____

3. her primary interest _____
   _____

4. enjoyed the taste of competition _____
   _____

Research Skills

Using the Internet, research cross-country ski racing to find out the answers to the following questions.

1. What are the types of races held at a cross-country competition?

2. What kind of equipment is used by a cross-country skier?

3. What are some problems a cross-country skier might encounter during a race?

Most Valuable Player — ★ Hayley Wickenheiser ★

Hayley Wickenheiser is considered the greatest female hockey player in the world. In 2003, Hayley was the first female player to score a point in a men's professional game when she played in the Finnish hockey league. Hayley was named the MVP of Canada's gold medal-winning team at both the 2002 Salt Lake City and 2006 Torino Winter Olympics. Her talent is unsurpassed.

Hayley Wickenheiser was born on August 12, 1978, in Shaunavon, Saskatchewan and is the oldest of three children. She learned to skate on a backyard rink, created by her parents, at the age of six. On this rink is where Hayley's love for hockey began. As a youngster, she played on a local boys' team and was the only girl. On many occasions, Hayley had to put on her gear in boiler rooms and other places in rinks as there often wasn't any available dressing rooms. It was a fight for her to enroll in a hockey school in Swift Current where, again, she was the only girl. Finally, her family moved to Calgary, Alberta so that she could play on an all-girls' team in the city. Hayley was a member of Team Alberta in the Canada Winter Games for the Under-17 Girls' Competition in 1991. At the competition, she helped her team to win a gold medal by scoring the winning goal and was named the MVP of the final game.

In 1994, at the age of 15, Hayley was chosen to play on Canada's National Women's Team. Her teammates who were much older nicknamed her "Highchair Hayley" because she was so young. During her first international tournament, at the 1994 World Championships in Lake Placid, her team won gold. In 1997, at her second World Championships her team captured the gold medal again and Hayley earned a spot on the tournament All-Star Team, which was the first of four times for her to be chosen. In 1999, Hayley helped Canada to win another gold medal and became the tournament MVP. Hayley has six World Championship gold medals and two silver medals. In 2001, she was named to play on Team Canada but had an injury and couldn't participate.

Hayley was a member of Team Canada at the 1998 Winter Olympics. This was the first time women's hockey was introduced as a sport. Canada won a silver medal and Hayley was named to the tournament all-star team.

In 2002, Hayley made the roster again for Team Canada and played in the Winter Olympics held in Salt Lake City, Utah. This time, Team Canada beat the United States in the final game and won the gold. In the Torino Olympics in Italy, Canada was defending its gold medal status against Sweden, a surprise finalist, and won. Hayley was named MVP, Top Forward, and awarded a place on the all-star team.

During her hockey career, Hayley continued her studies at the University of Calgary in its pre-med program. In 2000, she qualified for a spot on the Canadian womens' softball team and travelled to the 2000 Summer Olympics in Sydney, Australia. She was the second Canadian woman to ever compete in both Winter and Summer Olympics.

When Hayley finished her amateur hockey career, she began to play on professional hockey teams. She chose to play on European teams as the game is played more openly and is less physical. For a brief period of time, Hayley played on a team for Finland and then signed a contract to play for a Swedish men's league.

Hayley has always advised young hockey players to work hard, think smart, and to give no excuses in their sport. She has been an excellent role model and an athlete to admire. ★

Hayley Wickenheiser

Name: _____ Date: _____

Reading Skills

Number the events that have taken place in Hayley Wickenheiser's life in the correct order.

____ Since it was difficult for Hayley to play on an all-girl team, her family moved to the city of Calgary.

____ Hayley had to play on a boys' hockey team as there was no girls' team in the area.

____ In Shaunavon, Saskatchewan, on August 12, 1978, the Wickenheiser's welcomed a baby girl into their family and named her Hayley.

____ Hayley eventually turned professional and played hockey on European teams.

____ At Lake Placid, Hayley played in her first international competition, the 1994 World Championship, where her team won gold.

____ Hayley began playing hockey on her backyard rink, at the age of six.

____ In 1994, Hayley was picked to play on Canada's National Women's Team, at the age of 15.

____ Hayley was named MVP and Top Forward when Canada won the gold at the Torino Olympics in Italy in 2006.

____ In 1991, Hayley scored the winning goal at the Canada Winter Games for the Under-17 Girls' Competition and her team won a gold medal.

____ At the Salt Lake City Olympics, Hayley played on Team Canada when they won gold by defeating the United States.

Vocabulary Skills

A. Classify each group of words as antonyms (A), synonyms (S), and homonyms (H) on the line provided.

1. professional, amateur _____
2. brief, short _____
3. for, against _____
4. tournament, competition _____
5. currant, current _____
6. team, teem _____
7. won, beat _____
8. winning, losing _____
9. talent, ability _____
10. gear, equipment _____

B. Record the correct homonym in each sentence.

> role, roll   beat, beet   time, thyme
> team, teem   been, bean

1. Her _____ in the play was quite funny.
2. Team Canada _____ Team U.S.A. at the Salt Lake City Olympics.
3. My mother used some _____ to make her stew taste better.
4. Which _____ did you want to win gold at the Olympics?
5. The _____ that he planted grew into a huge plant.
6. Suddenly, the rain began to _____ down and we had to run fast to our car.
7. The boy pulled a large red _____ out of the garden.
8. "Where have you _____ all this time?" asked the boy's mother.
9. I watched as the ball began to _____ under the bed.
10. The old man checked the clock for the _____.

Show Jumping Champion ★ Beth Underhill ★

Beth Underhill is an accomplished athlete and one of the best known in the world of Canadian show jumping. She competes in a sport in which women are equal to men, and rides for the Canadian Show Jumping Team. With the help of her equine partners, she has been victorious during many equestrian events and competitions.

Beth was born in Guelph, Ontario on September 5, 1962. When she was seven, her parents enrolled her in riding lessons at a YMCA camp in Georgetown during the summer. At the age of 14, Beth joined the Toronto-North York Pony Club and learned the different forms of riding. She enjoyed the eventing, the games, and the dressage but was very intrigued with the sport of show jumping. At the age of 15, Beth decided to concentrate her efforts on it.

Due to their daughter's new passion, Beth's parents purchased a farm shortly after her competitive career was underway. During high school, Beth competed throughout Ontario at various show jumping events. After completing high school, Beth decided to sell her horse and move to Edmonton, Alberta to ride with Mark Larkin. While working with Larkin, she found a horse called Sagan, who was a veteran jumper. On Sagan, Beth learned to develop an eye for accuracy while having Sagan jump. If she got him to the right spot, he would jump anything but if their approach was wrong, Sagan would stop and Beth would fall off. Finally, patience and persistence won a grand prix for the rider and horse.

Beth returned to Ontario with Sagan and in 1984 and 1986, they won the Ontario Open Jumper Competitions. Eager to learn more, Beth took a job with Torchy Miller. During the 1989-1990 season Beth found Monopoly, a New Zealand thoroughbred. It took Beth months of training to get to know his personality and how they could be successful together.

In 1990, the team came together and during that summer, Beth and Monopoly won the $25,000.00 DuMaurier at Bromont, Quebec. During Monopoly's show jumping career, he won over $1 million dollars and was a star in the Canadian

show jumping world with a huge fan base. In 2001, Monopoly was retired and lives at Beth's stable.

Beth's partnership with Monopoly brought many opportunities and challenges her way. She became a sponsored rider as well as riding horses for various owners. In 1994, Beth tried out a horse in Europe called Altair. He was a Dutch warm blood who stood 16.3 hands high and Beth felt he was the most incredible horse that she had ever sat on. Altair was very expensive and Beth did not want to leave him behind, so she found investors to buy him and brought Altair to Canada.

Altair was a challenge to train and to get to know, but Beth did enjoy great success competing at the World Equestrian Games in Rome, in 1998. They were also a part of the Canadian team that won a bronze medal at the 1999 Pan American Games. In the same year, Altair and Beth finished second in the richest show jumping event in the world, the $800,000 Du Maurier International at the Spruce Meadows Masters Tournament, where Beth was also named the "Leading Lady Rider." During a show in Monterray, California, Altair suffered an injury and in 2006, following a sudden illness, had to be put down.

Beth now competes with Magdaline, a mare. Together, they have won several important events. Beth feels the life of a professional rider has its ups and downs but the thrill of competition and the partnership between horse and rider are very rewarding. ★

Beth Underhill

Name: _____ Date: _____

Reading Skills

1. In what ways is Beth Underhill's chosen sport different from most athletes? _____
   _____
   _____
   _____

2. What does an equestrian rider have to do with its equine partner before they can compete? _____
   _____
   _____

3. What qualities must a rider have in order to train a horse? _____
   _____
   _____
   _____

4. How successful was Beth Underhill with her horse Monopoly? _____
   _____
   _____
   _____

5. What further opportunities did Beth have after her partnership with Monopoly? _____
   _____
   _____
   _____

6. On which horse did Beth finish second in the richest show jumping event in the world? _____
   _____
   _____

7. How did Beth acquire Altair? _____
   _____
   _____
   _____

8. What would be some of the dangers a rider must be prepared to face during an event?
   _____
   _____
   _____

Vocabulary Skills

A. Record each word in the box on the line beside its meaning.

equine	equestrian	victorious
dressage	persistence	accuracy
eventing	thoroughbred	approach
investors	personality	intrigued

1. holding fast to a purpose _____
2. like a horse _____
3. qualities that make a person different _____
4. on horseback, mounted on a horse _____
5. pure breed or stock _____
6. equestrian competition _____
7. to excite one's curiosity _____
8. having no errors _____
9. having a victory, conquering _____
10. to come near or close _____
11. guidance of a horse through steps without the use of reins or noticeable signals _____
12. a person who invests money _____

B. Skim through the biography to locate antonyms for the following words.

1. cheap _____
2. stallion _____
3. poorest _____
4. cold _____
5. small _____
6. right _____
7. same _____
8. man _____

Canada's Tramp Champ — ★ Karen Cockburn ★

Karen Cockburn is a Canadian trampoline gymnast. She is a legend in the trampoline event and has been the best trampoline gymnast in Canada for 12 years. Since she has been on the national team, she has overcome many obstacles during her rise to the top of the trampoline world and has achieved national and international recognition. Her efforts have made her a great ambassador for Canada and the sport of trampoline.

Karen was born in Toronto on October 2, 1980 and was raised in the suburb called North York. Her athletic career began with the sport of diving. She used the trampoline during her training to simulate a diving board. At the age of 11, Karen switched from diving to artistic gymnastics. It was then that she realized the competitive trampoline was her true calling.

Karen was selected to join the Canadian National team when she was 14. One day, during training in 1995, Karen accidentally stepped on a ball while practising on the trampoline. She seriously injured her knee and had to have reconstructive surgery. Her injury kept her from training and competing for a year. She returned to the competitive trampoline world wearing a knee brace until 1999.

Karen developed a reputation throughout the trampoline world as being able to land her flips exactly where she planned on the trampoline. She also is known for her strong competitive drive that provides her with the energy to perform some of the most difficult routines in the world.

Karen has dominated the trampoline gymnastics sport in Canada, winning the national title nine times. In the 2000 Olympic Games held in Sydney, Karen came home with a bronze medal. Four years later in the Athens Olympic Games, she performed a difficult trampoline routine that secured her a birth in

the finals. She won a silver medal and was the first trampoline gymnast to win two Olympic medals.

In 2003, Cockburn won her first world title. Since then, she has won dozens of World Cup medals. Karen is also part of a world class women's synchronized trampoline team. Her partner is Rosannagh MacLennan and together they have won eight World Cups in a row and captured gold at the 2007 World Championships. At the 2008 Summer Olympics in Beijing, Karen qualified for the finals in 4th place and won a silver medal in the women's final. She is the only trampoline athlete to have won a medal at every Olympic Games. Karen was chosen to carry Canada's flag during the closing ceremonies of the Beijing Olympics.

Karen's accomplishments have brought many aspiring trampolinists to the various clubs in Canada and have helped with the recognition and awareness of the sport of trampolining.

On December 22, 2007 Karen married her fellow-Olympian and former training partner Mathieu Turgeon. Karen's biography, entitled Karen Cockburn: Flying High, was published in November of 2007. ✯

Karen Cockburn

Name: _____ Date: _____

Reading Skills

Answer each question with a complete sentence.

1. What special skill made Karen Cockburn a famous trampolinist?
   _____
   _____

2. Why is Karen Cockburn able to perform such difficult routines?
   _____
   _____

3. What previous sport introduced Karen to the trampoline?
   _____
   _____

4. How has Karen been an ambassador for the sport of trampolining?
   _____
   _____

5. In what other sport is Karen also involved?
   _____
   _____

6. How successful have Karen and Rosannagh been as a team?
   _____
   _____

7. How successful has Karen Cockburn been as a trampolinist?
   _____
   _____

8. What honour was Karen Cockburn given at the Beijing Olympics?
   _____
   _____

Vocabulary Skills

A. On the line provided, record the number of syllables that you hear in each word.

1. trampoline ____   6. recognition ____
2. international ____ 7. ceremonies ____
3. synchronized ____   8. obstacles ____
4. reconstructive ____ 9. competitive ____
5. ambassador ____   10. simulate ____

B. Skim through the biography and find a word that matches each of the following meanings.

1. an old story _____
2. used for tumbling _____
3. a type of operation _____
4. to act like _____
5. happened at the same time _____
6. someone's life story _____
7. rebuild _____
8. badly _____

Research Skills

Using the Internet or the resource centre, research to find out the answers to the following questions. Use these key words: trampoline, trampolining

1. Who invented the trampoline?
   _____

2. Where did the inventor get this idea?
   _____

3. What are the various moves and positions used by gymnasts on the trampoline?
   _____
   _____
   _____

A Man of Many Faces ★ Mike Myers ★

Mike Myers is a British Canadian actor, comedian, screenwriter, and film producer. He was born on May 25, 1965 in Liverpool, England. Later his family moved to Scarborough, Ontario, when he was quite young.

During his early years, Mike was immersed in British culture by his father. Together, they watched English movies and shows on televisions, such as the *James Bond Series*, *The Saint*, and *The Avengers*. Relatives from England often sent him things such as clothing, Beatle boots and even albums. His father loved comedy and humour as well and introduced Mike to The Goons, Peter Sellers' Inspector Clouseau, Peter Cook, Dudley Moore, and Monty Python. As Mike grew older, he relied on his father's response to a joke or funny story that he told. If his dad laughed, Mike knew his joke or story was good. The biggest thrill he had one day as a youngster was when he told a funny story and everyone in the house laughed.

Mike was a cute-looking kid and a natural for commercials on television. At the age of eight, Mike appeared in commercials for Pepsi Cola and Kit Kat. At the age of nine, he appeared in an ad for British Columbia Hydro. Gilda Radner, a star on *Saturday Night Live*, played his mother. *Saturday Night Live* eventually became one of Mike's favourite television shows.

Mike attended two high schools in Scarborough and was a fair student, but his interests were mainly in entertainment. As a teen, he took dance lessons and built a series of comic characters, some of which he still uses today. At parties, Mike was always trying to make girls laugh by playing one character who would later bring him monumental success. That character was called Wayne Campbell. After high school, Mike won a place with the *Second City* comedy troupe.

Second City was one of North America's most prestigious comedy groups. It had been formed in the early 1950s by a group of Chicago students. In 1973, a new branch was opened in Toronto featuring Dan Aykroyd, Gilda Radner, John Candy, Eugene Levy, and Catherine O'Hara. Mike Myers joined *Second City* in 1982, and it was here he received his first formal training in comedy.

Eventually, the lure of his native homeland, England, drew him back to his roots in the early 1980s. Mike teamed up with another comedian named Neil Mullarkey. Together, they performed sketches based on their love of cartoons, B-movies and bad television. In 1986, Mike returned to Toronto and *Second City* as a cast member in the main stage show. In 1988, Mike moved from *Second City* in Toronto to the one in Chicago. During his stay in Chicago, he made numerous appearances as Wayne Campbell and trained and performed at the *Improv Olympics*.

From 1989 to 1995, Mike was a member of the cast of NBC's *Saturday Night Live* where he performed characters such as Simon, Deiter, Linda Richman, and Wayne Campbell from *Wayne's World*. In 1992, Myers and comedian Dana Carvey adapted the Wayne's World sketch into a full-length movie. It turned out to be one of Myers' greatest successes.

Mike has starred in other movies, such as *So I Married an Axe Murderer*, *Austin Powers: International Man of Mystery*, *54*, *Austin Powers in Goldmember*, and *The Cat in the Hat*. In 2001, Myers played the lead role in the animated film *Shrek*, which was followed by *Shrek 3D*, *Shrek 2*, *Shrek the Third*, and the Christmas special *Shrek the Halls*. In 2008, his latest movie, *The Love Guru*, met with many negative reviews from movie critics as they did not feel it was funny.

Mike Myers is presently at the very top of the comedy world. It takes hard work and a vivid imagination to stay so high for so long. Mike will undoubtedly continue to invent new ways to make fun of himself and entertain his many fans. ★

Mike Myers

Name: _____ Date: _____

Reading Skills

A. When did each event take place in Mike Myers' life? Record the missing word on the line provided in each sentence.

> **before** or **after** or **during**

1. Mike Myers was born _____ he came to Canada.
2. Mike watched many British movies and television shows _____ his childhood with his father.
3. Mike joined *Second City* _____ he finished high school.
4. *Second City* was formed in Chicago _____ _____ the early 1950s.
5. *Second City* in Toronto was formed _____ _____ the one in Chicago.
6. _____ 1982, Mike began his training in comedy at *Second City*.
7. Myers performed in England with another comedian _____ 1989.
8. Mike always told his father a new joke _____ he told it to anyone else.
9. Several other animated movies about *Shrek* were made _____ the first one.
10. The movie *Wayne's World* was made _____ the time Mike was a cast member on *Saturday Night Live*.

B. Think of ten adjectives or phrases that describe Mike Myers.

_____
_____
_____
_____
_____

Vocabulary Skills

A. Match the words in the box to their meanings. Record each one on the line provided.

> immersed   culture   response
> natural   monumental   adapted
> animated   critic   thrill

1. an exciting feeling _____
2. a person who judges the work of others _____
3. lively, vigorous _____
4. to involve deeply _____
5. impressive; very great _____
6. customs of a nation _____
7. suitable _____
8. not man-made or artificial _____
9. an answer by word or act _____

B. Record the number of syllables heard in each word. Then divide them into syllables on the lines provided.

1. commercials   ___ _____
2. entertainment ___ _____
3. monumental   ___ _____
4. prestigious   ___ _____
5. animated   ___ _____
6. imagination   ___ _____
7. comedian   ___ _____
8. negative   ___ _____

An Aspiring Young Star — ★ Ryan Gosling ★

Ryan Gosling is a charming, attractive actor who has steadily developed an impressive film and television resume. He is the youngest of the two children in his family and was born on November 12, 1980 to Donna and Thomas Gosling in London, Ontario. He was raised in the small city of Cornwall, Ontario, where his father was a paper mill worker. During elementary school, Ryan was bullied by other students and was often involved in fights, so his mother decided to withdraw him from school and teach him at home. During his high school years, he went to Cornwall Collegiate and Vocational School and when his family relocated to Burlington, Ontario, he attended Lester B. Pearson High School. At the age of 17, Ryan dropped out of school and went to live in Los Angeles in 1997.

As a child, Ryan began his show business career with his older sister, Mandi, by participating in local talent shows. In 1993, at the age of 13, Ryan auditioned on a whim for the 1990's revival of *The Mickey Mouse Club* and beat out 17,000 aspiring young actors. This was his first acting experience and he was in the cast along with such superstars as Christina Aguilera, Britney Spears, Justin Timberlake, JC Chasez and Keri Russell. He spent two years taping episodes that aired over a four year period.

In 1995, while he was a teen, Ryan starred in the movie *Frankenstein and Me* and tried to bring the man-invented creature back to life on the Disney Channel. During the same year, he played a British foundling in an episode of *The Road to Avonlea,* which brought him a Gemini Award nomination. In 1997, Ryan played the role of a smooth-talking hypochondriac in *Breaker High,* which was a half-hour series about a high school set up on a cruise ship. In 1998, Gosling was cast in the television series *Young Hercules,* which earned him the status of a teen pin-up.

During the year 2000 on the big screen, Ryan was cast in the role of a football player on a squad that was coping with integration of the team in the true-life drama *Remember the Titans*. In 2001, Ryan played an intelligent, young Jewish teen who becomes involved with a neo-Nazi group in the film *The Believer*. In the movie *The Slaughter Rule,* filmed in 2002, Ryan was cast as another troubled teen trying to cope with life in a violent world. During the same year, he played a murderous teen who was trying to outwit an F.B.I. agent in the film *Murder by Numbers*.

Ryan played his first romantic role opposite Rachel Mc Adams in the popular film *The Notebook*, in 2004. *Stay* was a thriller in which Gosling played a suicidal patient in 2005. His next film *Half Nelson,* in 2006, showed Gosling as a serious actor on the rise. He gave a stellar performance as an idealistic and inspiring inner city teacher who has an after school drug habit. For his role in this film, he was nominated for an Academy Award for Best Actor. In 2007, Ryan played an ambitious Deputy D.A. in the courtroom thriller *Fracture,* along with acclaimed actor Anthony Hopkins.

During his acting career, Ryan has been nominated for many awards and has won several. He is the first Canadian born performer in over 60 years to be nominated for the Best Actor Oscar. During his career, Ryan has been described as the most consistent and compelling present day actor. The future looks very bright and promising for this young Canadian in the world of acting. ★

Ryan Gosling

Name: _____ Date: _____

Reading Skills

Ryan Gosling has played different roles in a number of television shows and movie theatre films. Read each clue and match the name of the movie or television show to which it pertains.

1. a true-life drama pertaining to integration
   _____

2. has a creature invented by a man
   _____

3. the set was on a cruise ship
   _____

4. involves anti-Semitism and youth
   _____

5. a teenager tries to prove that he is smarter than the law.
   _____

6. a young teacher aspires to change the world
   _____

7. takes place in a courtroom
   _____

8. a young person tries to cope with a violent world
   _____

9. earned Ryan the status of a teen pin-up
   _____

10. Ryan performed his first romantic leading role
    _____

11. This was his debut acting role.
    _____

12. deals with a person who is mentally ill
    _____

Vocabulary Skills

A. Match the words located in the box to their meanings. Record the word on the line provided.

attractive	charming	hypochondriac
impressive	foundling	integration
outwit	thriller	ambitious
compelling	whim	revival

1. charming; lovely; pleasing
   _____

2. seeking money, power or honours
   _____

3. pleasing qualities; fascinating; alluring
   _____

4. irresistible; overpower; force
   _____

5. making everything available to all races or groups
   _____

6. exciting emotion of admiration
   _____

7. a deserted baby without known parents
   _____

8. a person who worries about his or her health excessively
   _____

9. to trick; fool or baffle someone
   _____

10. something that causes a sudden feeling or excitement
    _____

11. a sudden or unexpected idea
    _____

12. a renewed interest in something done in the past
    _____

A Star With a Purpose — ★ Michael J. Fox ★

Michael J. Fox is a well-known film and television star, composer, director, writer, and producer in Canada and the United States. Michael was born in Edmonton, Alberta on June 9, 1961 as Michael Andrew Fox. While his father was involved with the military, his family moved about and lived in various places, but later settled in Burnaby, British Columbia. Michael was the youngest of five children.

As a youngster, Michael loved hockey and dreamed of a career in the National Hockey League but his small stature of 5'5" was against him ever becoming a hockey player. When Michael was eight, he received his first guitar for Christmas and taught himself how to play it. During his teenage years, he played the guitar with a series of rock and roll garage bands. At this stage in his life, his interests expanded to experimenting with creative writing and art. He also quit attending Burnaby South Secondary School before he graduated, which he now regrets, claiming it was "a stupid youth mistake".

In 1979, Michael debuted as a professional actor when he co-starred in the Canadian sitcom *Leo and Me* on CBC at the age of 15. For three years, he worked at local theatres, did TV work, and landed the occasional role in American TV movies that were being filmed in Canada. Finally at the age of 18, Michael moved to Los Angeles to pursue an acting career. His television movie debut was *Letters from Frank*. When he went to register his name with the Screen Actors Guild, he discovered that there was a veteran character actor with the same name. Since the Screen Actors Guild does not allow duplicate names to be registered, Michael needed to come up with a different name. He decided to adopt a new initial which was the letter J, in reference to character actor Michael J. Pollard.

Michael also landed parts in the Disney movie *Midnight Madness* and the weekly drama *Palmerston, U.S.A.* He also made appearances on popular television shows, such as *Trapper John M.D.* and the *Love Boat*. It seemed that Michael was off to a great start until *Palmerston, U.S.A.* was cancelled in 1981. Michael's luck began a downward decline. He had been living the good life, spending money, and was in debt. He had to sell some of his possessions and moved into a garage apartment where he lived on macaroni and cheese. Feeling unwell and depressed, he was considering going home. He decided to have one more crack at acting and auditioned for the role of Alex P. Keaton, the arrogant, wise-cracking teenager on the television series *Family Ties* and got the part.

The show became one of the most adored and highly rated sitcoms of the 1980's. During its seven years on television, Michael J. Fox won three Emmy Awards and one Golden Globe Award for his portrayal of Alex P. Keaton, making him one of the country's most prominent young actors. Michael shot to movie stardom in the mid-1980s with his leading role as time traveller Marty McFly in the *Back to the Future* trilogy of films. Some of his other notable films are *Teen Wolf*; *The Secret of My Success*; *Bright Lights, Big City*; *Doc Hollywood*; *The Hard Way*; *For Love or Money*; *Life With Mikey*; *Greedy*; *The American President*; and *Mars Attack*. His last major film was *The Frighteners* in 1996.

From 1996 to 2001, Michael played the role of Mike Flaherty, the deputy Mayor of New York City, in the sitcom *Spin City*. While on the set, Michael often put his right hand in his pocket to hide the tremors that were occurring. In 1990, while filming a movie, Michael noticed a tremor in his little finger which didn't go away. After consulting a doctor, he was diagnosed with young on-set Parkinson's Disease In 1998, Michael decided to go public with the condition and left *Spin City* in January.

Today, Michael still does some acting or lends his voice to characters in movies as the symptoms of his disease are controlled by medication. His main focus is on the Michael J. Fox Foundation for Parkinson's Research, which he created. His efforts and strength in attempting to conquer this debilitating disease have attracted many celebrities and the admiration of thousands of people. ★

Michael J. Fox

Name: _____   Date: _____

Reading Skills

Answer each question with a complete sentence on the lines provided.

1. What was the career Michael J. Fox dreamed of having as a child?

2. What decision did Michael make in the past that he later claimed was a big mistake?

3. Why was it necessary for Michael to change his name?

4. How do you know Michael did not plan for the future?

5. What role and television sitcom made Michael J. Fox famous?

6. How do you know Michael was a success on *Family Ties* as an actor?

7. When did Michael notice there was something wrong with him?

8. What is the name of the disease that Michael J. Fox has?

9. How did Michael hide his disease at first?

10. What is the most important event that Michael would like to see happen in the future?

Vocabulary Skills

Match each word in the box to its meaning. Record each one on the line provided.

stature	register	reference	trilogy
symptom	veteran	prominent	pursue
guild	duplicate	debilitate	conquer

1. to weaken or to make feel feeble

2. pointing out or referring to

3. a sign or indication that something is wrong

4. to record or enter in a book

5. well known; important

6. someone who has had a great deal of experience

7. a group of three literary compositions on the same subject

8. a group of persons with the same interests

9. to follow; to seek to attain

10. double or repeat in the same manner

Research Skills

Michael J. Fox has a debilitating disease called young on-set Parkinson's Disease. Use the Internet research to find out the symptoms of the disease and how it affects someone's body. Record the facts in a paragraph in your notebook.

Handsome Leading Man — ★ Matthew Perry ★

Matthew Perry is best known for his role as Chandler Bing in the very popular sitcom *Friends,* which played on television for ten years. Matthew Langford Perry was born on August 19, 1969 in Williamstown, Massachusetts. His mother is Suzanne Jane Louise Morrison, a Canadian journalist and past press secretary to former Canadian Prime Minister Pierre Trudeau. His father is John Bennett Perry, an American actor and former model. His parents divorced before he was a year old, and Matthew was raised by his mother in Ottawa, Ontario. Matthew attended Rockcliffe Park Public School, Lisgar Collegiate Institute, and Ashbury College.

While he was growing up in Ottawa, Matthew became a talented tennis player and at the age of 13, was ranked as number two among the junior players in Canada. In the same year, he discovered acting when he played a role in a seventh grade production called *The Life and Death of Sneaky Fitch*. When he was 15, Matthew decided to move to Los Angeles to live and spend more time with his father. During his teenage years, he became involved in the drama program at Buckley School in Sherman Oaks and appeared in the plays *Our Town, The Miracle Worker,* and *The Sound of Music*. After giving up on his dreams of becoming a famous tennis player, Matthew got his professional break at the age of 18 by being cast in the movie *A Night in the Life of Jimmy Reardon,* with River Phoenix.

Matthew also pursued improv comedy at the L.A. Connection in Sherman Oaks, while in high school, and quickly became a featured performer. After graduating from high school, Matthew planned on enrolling at the University of Southern California, but was offered the lead role of Chazz Russell in the television series *Second Chance,* in 1987. The show only ran for one season and when it finished, Matthew made guest appearances on television programs such as *Growing Pains* and *Beverly Hills 90210*.

In 1990, on the CBS sitcom called *Sydney,* Perry played the younger brother of Valerie Bertinelli. Three years later, he landed a starring role on the ABC sitcom *Homefree,* but the show only lasted for 13 episodes. Matthew was gradually making his mark in acting and was cast this time in a new dramatic pilot called *LAX 2194*. Since this project was slow to take off, Matthew auditioned for a new sitcom called *Friends* and got the part of Chandler Bing. This show was extremely successful and Perry and his co-stars became famous.

Perry has also appeared in various films, such as *Fools Rush In,* with his father John Bennett Perry, *Almost Heroes*, *Three to Tango*, *The Whole Nine Yards* with Bruce Willis, and its sequel *The Whole Ten Yards*, and *Serving Sara*. Matthew is known primarily for his comedic roles, but has displayed talent in the dramatic side of acting as well, especially in his role as Joe Quincy in *West Wing* and as an attorney in two episodes of *Ally McBeal*. In 2006, Perry starred in the movie *The Ron Clark Story,* where he plays a small town teacher who teaches the toughest class in the country.

During his career, Matthew has experienced many highs and lows and has endured personal problems as well. He has suffered from several addictions and has been in and out of rehabilitation centres in the last few years. Hopefully, Matthew will overcome his problems and will continue to present his wonderful talent to entertain stage, film, and television audiences. ★

Matthew Perry

Name: _____ Date: _____

Reading Skills

Circle the correct answer for each question about Matthew Perry.

1. In which city was Matthew Perry raised as a young child?

   Orono   Oshawa   Ottawa   Orangeville

2. In which state was Matthew Perry born?

   Maine   Missouri   Montana   Massachusetts

3. In which sport was Matthew talented?

   hockey   tennis   lacrosse   baseball

4. Which television series brought him and its cast fame?

   Second Chance   Sydney
   Friends   Homefree

5. In which genre of acting is Matthew mainly cast?

   drama   tragedy
   comedy   music and dance

6. In which movie did Matthew and his father both have roles?

   Almost Heroes   Fools Rush In   Serving Sara

7. What was the role Matthew played in episodes of *Ally McBeal*?

   teacher   actor   doctor   attorney

8. What was the name of Matthew's character in *Friends*?

   Chandler Bing   Chazz Russell   Jimmy Reardon

9. For how many years was the sitcom *Friends* popular on television?

   six   ten   one   three

10. How old was Matthew when he went to live with his father?

    twenty   nineteen   ten   fifteen

Vocabulary Skills

A. Using a straight line, match the words in both columns that are antonyms.

1. married •   • nightmare
2. dream •   • enemies
3. professional •   • senior
4. comedy •   • tragedy
5. lead •   • finished
6. friends •   • amateur
7. began •   • divorced
8. junior •   • follow

B. Match each word in the box to its synonym. Record it on the line provided.

lifted	hardest	throw
found	primarily	endured
registering	difficulties	lawyer

1. raised _____
2. discovered _____
3. enrolling _____
4. mainly _____
5. problems _____
6. cast _____
7. lasted _____
8. attorney _____
9. toughest _____

Canada's Comic Film Star ★ Jim Carrey ★

Jim Carrey has been the driving force behind some of the most successful comedy films of all time. He is perhaps the most successful of the Canadians who have gone to Hollywood and made good. Carrey is well known for his frightening manic attack, his flexible rubber face, and his boundless appetite for excess. He has won six Golden Globes, 22 MTV Movie Awards (the most by any one actor in MTV history), a Screen Actors Guild Award, two People's Choice Awards, and a star on Canada's Walk of Fame.

Carrey was born James Eugene Carrey on January 17, 1962, in Newmarket, Ontario. His parents were Kathleen and Percy Carrey and he is the youngest of four siblings. As a child, Jim became a serious extrovert who seized every opportunity to entertain his family or anyone he could find. At the age of ten, he sent a book of poetry to a publisher to be published and a résumé to the producers of *The Carol Burnett Show*. During high school, his teachers granted him ten minutes at the end of each day to do stand-up routines for his friends, provided that he had behaved during the rest of the day.

During Carrey's teens, his family was obliged to move from Newmarket to Scarborough, since his father had lost his job, and forced to sell their home. In order to make ends meet, the entire family took jobs as security guards or janitors at the Titan Wheel factory. Jim also had to work an eight hour shift after school scrubbing toilets and cleaning certain areas. This experience made him very determined to escape to a better life.

At 16, Jim dropped out of high school altogether and began to work on his act as a stand-up comic, as he was determined to have a career in show business. His father, who was somewhat of a comedian, helped Jim write his first routines. Carrey made his debut at Yuk Yuk's comedy club, dressed in a yellow polyester suit with tails made by his mother. His first show was a disaster and embarrassing, but Jim was not deterred and carried on performing at Toronto clubs, perfecting his impressions of various movie stars.

In 1979, Jim relocated to Los Angeles in the hopes of hitting the big times. He became a regular at The Comedy Store where he was spotted by Rodney Dangerfield, who took him on tour as his support act for a season. Shortly afterwards, Carey was offered the role of a novice cartoonist in the series *The Duck Factory*, which lasted for only 13 episodes. This experience gave Carrey the confidence to pursue acting more seriously. In 1985, he scored the male lead in the film *Once Bitten* and a supporting role in *Peggy Sue Got Married* in 1986, as well as a modest appearance as the Alien Wiploc in *Earth Girls Are Easy* (1989).

In 1990, Carrey joined the cast of *In Living Colour* and made a name for himself with his outrageous acts, which transformed him from TV goofball to a marquee headline in a single year. In 1994, Carrey starred in *Ace Ventura: Pet Detective*, a film that cashed in on his physical brand of humour. That same year, he performed as a manic superhero in the movie *The Mask*, in which Carrey's ability to stretch his facial features surprised audiences. A few months later in December, Carrey hit theatres as a loveable numbskull in *Dumb and Dumber*. Carrey had finally become a box-office staple with his first multi-million dollar making movie. In 1995, he brought his manic antics to the movie *Batman Forever* as The Riddler. In 1996, Jim was to star in *The Cable Guy* for a cool $20 million, which was the biggest upfront sum ever offered any comic actor. Although this movie was a financial disappointment, Carrey bounced back in 1997 with the energy filled movie *Liar, Liar*. In 1998, Carrey was worried that his comedy routines would soon wear thin so he decided to participate in more serious productions such as *The Truman Show* (1999), and *Man in the Moon* (1999). During the Year 2000, he also slipped into the furry green suit of The Grinch to star in the movie *How the Grinch Stole Christmas*.

In 2004, Carrey became an American citizen and, at that time, he made it very clear that he had no intention of giving up his Canadian heritage and was proud to be a Canadian. After years of struggling and self doubt, Jim Carrey has finally arrived at the top of his career. He is now considered the world's premier comedian and will likely have that distinction for years to come. ★

Jim Carrey

Name: _____   Date: _____

Reading Skills

Locate the answer to each question in the biography and record it on the line provided.

1. In which movie does Jim Carrey wear a furry, green suit?
   _____

2. Where did Jim Carrey make his stand-up comic debut?
   _____

3. How was Jim dressed for his debut performance?
   _____

4. In which club, in Los Angeles, did Carrey play as a regular stand-up comic?
   _____

5. With whom did Jim Carrey go on tour?
   _____

6. What is the name of the series in which Carrey was to play a cartoonist?
   _____

7. In which film did Carrey display his ability to stretch his facial features?
   _____

8. What type of character role did Jim play in the movie Dumb and Dumber?
   _____

9. What role did Carrey play in Batman Forever?
   _____

10. For which movie was Carrey paid $20 million dollars up front?
    _____

Vocabulary Skills

A. Match the words in the box to their meanings. Record the words on the lines provided.

manic	predecessor	goofball
extrovert	polyester	numbskull
marquee	outrageous	staple

1. something or someone who comes before
   _____

2. a stupid person; blockhead; idiot
   _____

3. main ingredient or element
   _____

4. a synthetic, wrinkle-free material
   _____

5. insane, great excitement
   _____

6. crazy or silly person
   _____

7. a person who tends to act before he thinks
   _____

8. a roof over the entrance of a theatre
   _____

9. shocking or bad behaviour
   _____

B. On the line, under each sentence, record the name of each part of speech that is underlined.

1. As a child, Jim Carrey became a serious extrovert. _____

2. Jim dressed in a yellow polyester suit.
   _____

3. He became a regular at The Comedy Store.
   _____

4. As the Grinch, Jim wore a funny green furry suit. _____

5. His entire family took jobs as security guards or janitors. _____

A Man of Mystery — ★ Keanu Reeves ★

Keanu Reeves is an avid fan of ice hockey, American football, surfing, table tennis, and soccer. He also enjoys riding the many motorcycles that he has collected. Keanu is a prolific reader and loves to play the bass guitar. Keanu Charles Reeves was born on September 2, 1964, in Beirut, Lebanon. His mother, Patricia Taylor, is a costume designer and is of English heritage. His father, Samuel Nowlin Reeves Jr. was a geologist and is an American of Hawaiian-Chinese and Irish-Portuguese heritage. Reeves' first name, Keanu, is pronounced "keh-ah-noo" and means "cool breeze over the mountains" in Hawaiian. Keanu had a very unstable childhood as his father abandoned the family when he was 13. His mother moved about frequently and has been married several times. Keanu had numerous stepfathers and does not have a relationship with his real father. Keanu and his sisters were raised by grandparents, nannies, and babysitters, and grew up primarily in Toronto.

In a span of five years, Keanu attended four different high schools, including the Etobicoke School of the Arts, from which he was expelled for being mouthy and rambunctious. During his high school years, he excelled more in hockey than in academics and often dreamed of becoming an Olympic hockey player. His academic growth was affected by dyslexia and his attitude towards learning. He dropped out of school before he graduated to pursue an acting career.

Keanu began his acting career, at the age of nine, when he appeared in the stage production *Damn Yankees*. At the age of 15, he played Mercutio in a stage production of *Romeo and Juliet*. His screen acting debut came in a CBC television comedy series called *Hangin' In*. During the 1980s, Keanu appeared in television commercials and shot films such as *One Step Away* and *Wolf Boy* in Toronto. In 1986, Keanu had his first studio movie appearance in Rob Lowe's ice hockey movie, *Youngblood*. It was filmed in Canada and Keanu played a Quebecois goalie. After the release of this movie, Keanu set out for Los Angeles in his 1969 Volvo. On his trip down to California, one of his stepfathers, who was a movie director, hired an agent to help him get roles in various movies. In 1986, after playing a few minor roles, Reeves got a sizable part in the movie *River's Edge*. During the late 1980s, he appeared in a number of movies aimed at teenage audiences such as *Permanent Record*, the comedy *Bill & Ted's Excellent Adventure*, and its 1991 sequel *Bill & Ted's Bogus Journey*. In both movies, Reeves was cast as a sweet-natured, lovable buffoon and it took Keanu a number of years to get rid of this image put upon him by the press.

During the 1990s, he began appearing in high-budget action films, such as *Point Break*, for which he won MTV's "Most Desirable Male" award in 1992. Keanu received good reviews for the low-budget independent film *My Own Private Idaho*, appearing alongside his good friend River Phoenix. In 1994, Keanu starred in the action thriller *Speed*, which helped his career reach a higher level. In this film, he was the sole headliner and it put him into the A-List of stars. In 1994, Keanu also scored a hit as a romantic leading man in the movie *A Walk in the Clouds*. Unfortunately, his movies *Johnny Mnemonic*, *Chain Reaction*, and *Feeling Minnesota* were declared disasters by critics and audiences.

In the movie *The Devil's Advocate*, Keanu starred with Al Pacino and Charlize Theron. The movie received good reviews and Keanu's career began to climb again. This movie also proved that Keanu could play a more grown-up, serious role. In 1999, *The Matrix* won him the status as an international superstar. He also received positive reviews for the movies *The Gift*, *The Matrix Reloaded*, *The Matrix Revolutions*, *Something's Gotta Give*, and *Constantine*.

For a number of years, Reeves preferred to live in rented homes and hotels. In 2003, he finally bought his first home in Hollywood Hills in Los Angeles and also maintains an apartment in New York. Keanu has never married and likes to keep his private life a mystery. ☆

Keanu Reeves

Name: _____ Date: _____

Reading Skills

Answer the following questions with complete sentences.

1. Keanu Reeves had a very unstable childhood. List the factors that contributed to this situation.
   _____
   _____
   _____
   _____

2. At what skill did Keanu excel during his high school years?
   _____
   _____
   _____

3. What affected his academic progress during high school?
   _____
   _____

4. In which movie do you think Keanu most enjoyed acting? Tell why.
   _____
   _____
   _____

5. In which films did movie critics have Keanu typecast as a lovable buffoon?
   _____
   _____
   _____

6. The comments and criticisms made by critics and the press can often damage an actor's career. Do you agree or disagree with this statement? State your feelings.
   _____
   _____
   _____
   _____

7. Keanu preferred to live in rented places, has never married and keeps his private life a mystery. Why do you think he has adopted this type of lifestyle?
   _____
   _____
   _____

Vocabulary Skills

A. Match the words in the box to their meanings. Record each word on the line provided.

rambunctious	prolific	unstable
abandoned	geologist	dyslexia
academics	desirable	advocate
matrix	buffoon	mnemonic

1. _____: art of improving or developing the money
2. _____: producing many offspring; fertile; having many
3. _____: a person knowledgeable with the science of the earth's crust
4. _____: not firmly fixed; easily moved or shaken
5. _____: to give up entirely; leave without returning
6. _____: wild and uncontrollable; unruly
7. _____: scholastic; to do with learning
8. _____: the inability to read properly
9. _____: worth wanting; worth having; pleasing; good
10. _____: to recommend publicly; to support
11. _____: something that gives form to something enclosed within it
12. _____: a person who amuses people with tricks, pranks, jokes; a clown

Research Skills

Using the Internet, research what causes dyslexia and how it affects people.
_____
_____
_____
_____
_____

Born to Act — ★ Kiefer Sutherland ★

Kiefer William Frederick Dempsey George Rufus Sutherland was born on December 21, 1966, in London, England while his parents were working there. Kiefer's father is the screen legend, Donald Sutherland, and his mother is the popular stage and television actress Shirley Douglas. He is also the grandson of one of Canada's most famous and influential politicians, Tommy Douglas, who was the Premier of Saskatchewan and the founder of socialized medicine. Kiefer has a twin sister named Rachel, and three half brothers.

When Kiefer and his sister were six, their parents moved to Corona, California in 1972. Shortly afterwards, his parents divorced and he moved to Toronto with his mother, where he attended school. Kiefer often spent time in the theatre, in which his mother was working, and occasionally visited his father on movie sets, where he was working. At the age of nine, he started holding acting workshops at his school. In high school, Kiefer was a track star and ended up being one of the top runners in Ontario.

At the age of 15, Kiefer got caught up in the acting world and began to perform at various youth theatres in Toronto. He eventually dropped out of school to pursue an acting career. His early acting credits were a walk-on that his father gave him in *Max Dugan Returns,* and the lead role in the Canadian film *The Bay Boy*. After this film, Kiefer decided to take off for the big time in New York City with some friends. The group rented an apartment and, within days, Kiefer was offered a part in a soap opera with a salary of $100,000 a year. Preferring to act in movies or on the stage, Kiefer turned down the offer and had no work for a year, even though he had hired an agent.

After a year of disappointment, Kiefer decided to head out on his own in his 1969 Mustang called Lucy, and drove to Los Angeles. Arriving in Los Angeles broke, Kiefer was forced to live on a beach for three months in his car, taking advantage of the public showers. In the late 1980s, he appeared in a series of hit movies. His bad boy look and personal magnetism made him a perfect choice for rough and tough roles as a gang leader in *Stand By Me,* head vampire in *The Lost Boys,* and Doc in *Young Guns.*

In 1990, Sutherland starred in the hit film *Flatliners* with Julia Roberts. In the movie, both actors are doctors experimenting with death. During 1992, Kiefer had a role in *A Few Good Men,* and appeared in *The Three Musketeers* in 1993. After these movies, Sutherland left Hollywood and spent time fine-tuning his rodeo skills on a ranch in Montana. Kiefer needed a break from acting and the types of films he had made, which he felt were not good ones. He needed time to figure out what he wanted to do with his life.

In 1993, Kiefer returned to direct and star as an immate on death row in the television drama *Last Night*, which was well received by the critics. In 1997, Kiefer starred and directed his first major motion picture *Truth or Consequences, N.M.* During the same year, he starred in the science-fiction film *Dark City,* which had good reviews, and was followed by his second self-directed TV movie, *Woman Wanted*. For a break, Kiefer returned to his theatrical roots with his mother in the Canadian production of *The Glass Menagerie* at the Royal Alexandra Theatre in Toronto.

For a while, Kiefer took supporting roles in higher profile films, as villains with very cruel intentions, in movies such as *An Eye for an Eye*, *A Time to Kill* and *Freeway*. In 1998, dissatisfied with his career and the work he was doing, Kiefer returned to the rodeo circuit. For two years, he travelled about competing in various rodeos, achieving great success. He loved the discipline and the entire experience. After a two year hiatus from acting, Kiefer returned to Hollywood rested and eager to make films again. One of his director friends encouraged him to try out for the role of Jack Bauer in the new television series *24*. His role as the powerful terrorism agent has earned him recognition as the Best Actor in a TV drama at the 2001 Golden Globe Awards, and the 2004 and 2006 Screen Actor's Guild Awards. Today, Kiefer is the highest paid actor in a TV drama and the series has continued to play for seven seasons. ☆

Kiefer Sutherland

Name: _____ Date: _____

Reading Skills

Complete each sentence carefully.

1. Kiefer Sutherland quit school at 15 because _____

2. His role in the television series *24* brought him fame and fortune because _____

3. Kiefer Sutherland was born in London, England, because _____

4. Kiefer has natural acting skills because _____

5. Kiefer is related to the famous Canadian politician, Tommy Douglas, because _____

6. When Kiefer first went to Los Angeles, his car was his home because _____

7. In his early movies, he played rough, tough roles because _____

8. Kiefer left Hollywood in 1993, and went to a ranch in Montana because _____

9. Kiefer liked to participate in rodeos because _____

10. Kiefer turned down the money and the role in the soap opera because _____

Vocabulary Skills

A. Using a dictionary, find out the meanings for the following words. Record them on the lines provided.

1. menagerie _____
2. theatrical _____
3. influential _____
4. socialized _____
5. magnetism _____
6. musketeer _____
7. consequences _____
8. hiatus _____
9. terrorism _____
10. agent _____

B. Classify the following words in the box on the syllable chart.

> consequences   experimenting   menagerie
> theatrical   production   intentions
> occasionally   terrorism   eventually
> apartment   influential   dissatisfied

Three Syllables

_____
_____
_____
_____

Four Syllables

_____
_____
_____
_____

Five Syllables

_____
_____
_____
_____

One of Canada's Treasures — ★ Sarah Polley ★

Sarah Polley is a Canadian actress, singer, screenwriter, and director. She is the youngest of five children and was born on January 8, 1979 in Toronto, Ontario into a show business family. Her mother, Diane Polley, was also an actress and casting director. Her father, Michael Polley, is a British actor and an insurance agent. Her older brother Mark is an actor and her second brother John is a casting director and producer.

Sarah's acting career began at the age of four, due to her mother's connections and her persistence to act. In 1985, Sarah played the role of Molly in the Disney film *One Magic Christmas*. In 1988, at the age of eight, Sarah was cast in the title role in the television series *Ramona*, which was based on Beverly Cleary's books. The series only lasted one season. As a child actress, her career took a dramatic change in 1990 when she was cast as the Cockney orphan Jody Turner in *Lantern Hill*, a television film. The film was based on the book written by Lucy Maud Montgomery. Sarah's efforts were rewarded with a Gemini Award in 1992. During the same year, Sarah had the opportunity to be in the public eye by appearing as Sara Stanley on the popular CBC television series *Road to Avonlea*. This series made her famous and financially independent and she was loved and adored by thousands of Canadian fans.

When Sara was 11, tragedy struck her family. Her mother, Diane Polley, died from cancer. This tragic event paralleled the life of the character Sara Stanley, who she was playing in the *Road to Avonlea*. Her mother's death made a great impact on her personal life. Being extremely intelligent and politically progressive, Sarah rebelled against the Americanization of the series when it was picked up by the Disney Channel. When Sara was 12, she attended an awards ceremony wearing a peace sign in protest of the first Gulf War. She was asked to remove it by Disney officials and she refused. Her relationship with Disney was not the same after the incident and she left *Road to Avonlea* in 1994. Sarah has often stated that she lost her childhood to her acting career. Although she does not blame her parents, she has said during interviews that she would never let any of her children act at an early age.

During her teens, Sarah attended the Subway Academy II, which was then called Earl Haig Secondary School. She became politically active, became a prominent member of the New Democratic Party, and dropped out of school before graduating. During a political protest at Queen's Park in Toronto in 1995,

Sarah lost several back teeth during a clash between the police and the protesters.

In 1996, Sara appeared as Lily on the CBC television series, *Straight Up*. It ran for two seasons and she won the Gemini Award for Best Performance in a Children's Series. Her next role was as Nicolle Burnelli, a teenager who was injured in a school bus accident, in the film *The Sweet Hereafter*. This role brought her attention from American and Canadian critics and was her breakthrough into adult roles.

In 1999, Sarah played a young woman named Harper who comes from a well-to-do family in the film *Guinevere*. She finds life boring and unfulfilling, and does not want to attend university. This film brought Sarah unwanted attention and fame, which was something she dislikes intensely, as she is an extremely private person. Sarah often rebels against the expected ways the media and critics feel one should accept celebrity and fame. As a result, she dropped out of the movie *Almost Famous* which was to make her a mainstream star in the United States and returned to Canada to make less money to do the film *The Law of Enclosures* in 2000.

For a period of time, Sarah took a wide variety of parts in independent films. Her choice of roles helped her to focus on the art of her craft and she also wanted to be in films with a social importance. ★

Sarah Polley

Name: _____ Date: _____

Reading Skills

In Sarah Polley's biography, locate the name of the film that each clue is describing. Record its title on the line provided.

1. This series ran for two seasons on television and Sarah won a Gemini Award for her performance.
   _____

2. In this television film, Sarah played the role of Jody Turner, a Cockney orphan.
   _____

3. Her role in this film, as Nicolle Burnelli, brought her attention from the United States.
   _____

4. Lucy Maud Montgomery wrote the book on which this television series was based.
   _____

5. At the age of four, she acted in her first Disney television film.
   _____

6. Her role in the film brought fame that she felt invaded her privacy.
   _____

7. This series was based on the books written by Beverly Cleary.
   _____

8. This film had been designed to make Sarah a popular star in the United States.
   _____

9. During this film series, Sarah showed a rebellious, political, and activist side to her personality.
   _____

Vocabulary Skills

A. Using a straight line connect each word to its meaning.

1. persistence •   • a surrounded area
2. cockney •   • extreme force; overpowering
3. tragedy •   • life after death
4. paralleled •   • like no other
5. hereafter •   • perserverance; lasting
6. enclosure •   • extremely sad event
7. ultimate •   • an English dialect
8. intensely •   • correspond to, similar

B. In the biography, locate synonyms for each of the following words. Record each one on the line provided.

1. waif _____
2. conflict _____
3. honoured _____
4. lamp _____
5. impression _____
6. clever _____
7. important _____
8. start _____

C. Record the root word for each of the following words on the line provided.

1. famous _____
2. business _____
3. actress _____
4. persistence _____
5. financially _____
6. progressive _____

ISBN: 9781554950898      48   SSJ1-78 • Female Actors

Blond and Beautiful — ★ Kim Cattrall ★

Kim Victoria Cattrall was born on August 21, 1956 in Widnes, England. Her mother, Shane, was a secretary and her father, Dennis, was a construction engineer. When Kim was less than a year old, her family emigrated to Courtenay, British Columbia. Kim is one of four children in the family. At the age of 11, Kim returned to England when her grandmother became ill. While she was there, Kim studied at the London Academy of Music and Dramatic Art. Kim returned to Canada when she was 16 and finished her final year of high school.

In 1972, after graduating from high school, Kim decided to pursue a career in acting and left Canada for New York City. Kim attended the America Academy of Dramatic Arts and, when she graduated, she was signed to a five year movie contract with world famous director Otto Preminger. She made her debut in his film *Rosebud* in 1975. A year later, her contract was bought by Universal Studios and Kim guest starred in various types and styles of television programs.

Her television work paid off and she began to work in various screen and television movies. In 1979, Kim was cast in the role of Dr. Gabrielle White in the film *The Incredible Hulk*. In 1980, Kim was part of the cast in the Oscar-nominated movie *Tribute*. The following year Kim played the role of Ruthie who was a member of a religious cult in *Ticket to Heaven*. During 1982, Kim played a physical education teacher, Miss Honeywell, in the comedy film *Porky's*. Two years later, Kim landed a role in the original *Police Academy*, where she plays Cadet Karen Thompson, who is training to become a police officer.

During 1985, Kim starred in three movies. In *Turk 182*, Kim plays a social worker trying to help an injured firefighter; in *City Limits*, she plays a character involved in a gang war; and in *Hold-up*, Kim plays the role of a hostage during a bank robbery in Montreal. In 1986, Kim played lawyer Gracie Law in the film *Big Trouble in Little China*. Kim was cast in the lead role as a store mannequin who comes to life magically to help a struggling artist in the movie *Mannequin*. This film was a successful comedy popular with many audiences.

One of Kim's best known film roles is that of the traitor Lieutenant Valeris in *Star Trek VI: The Undiscovered Country* in 1991. Kim has also acted on the stage doing plays, and uses these opportunities as a break from making films. She has had important roles in the plays *A View from the Bridge* and *Three Sisters*.

In 1997, Kim was cast in the television series *Sex and the City* as Samantha Jones, a public relations executive. This television series brought her international recognition. *Sex and the City* ended as a weekly series in the spring of 2004. In the Disney production of *Ice Princess*, which was filmed in 2005, Kim played the role of Tina Harwood an ice skating coach. Unfortunately, this film was not a financial success at the box office. In the same year, Kim played the role of a woman who is paralyzed and wants to die in the theatre production *Whose Life Is It Anyway?* in London, England. She also was cast in the play *The Cryptogram* at the Donmar Warehouse in London. While Kim was acting in London, she also appeared in a number of Tetley Tea and Nissan car commercials for British television and acted in several films that did not do well at the box office.

Kim Cattrall is an actress who has been nominated 20 times for various awards for acting on television. During her career, she has won awards for four of the nominations. ★

Kim Cattrall

Name: _____   Date: _____

Reading Skills

Locate the name of the movie to match the character played by Kim Cattrall. Record each one on the line provided.

1. a physical education teacher
   _____

2. a girl named Ruthie
   _____

3. a social worker
   _____

4. a store mannequin
   _____

5. Lieutenant Valeris
   _____

6. an ice skating coach
   _____

7. Cadet Karen Thompson
   _____

8. Dr. Gabrielle White
   _____

9. a hostage in a building
   _____

10. Gracie Law, a lawyer
    _____

Vocabulary Skills

A. Use each group of words to help form a good sentence about Kim Cattrall.

1. stage, television, film
   _____
   _____

2. studied, dramatic, academy
   _____
   _____

3. high school, pursue, career
   _____
   _____

4. poor, films, box office
   _____
   _____

B. Record each group of words in the correct alphabetical order on the line provided.

1. executive, engineer, education, emigrated
   _____
   _____

2. styles, studied, studios, signed
   _____
   _____

3. dramatic, debut, die, director
   _____
   _____

4. movie, magically, member, many
   _____
   _____

5. finished, final, financial, family
   _____
   _____

A Bright, Shining Star

★ Neve Campbell ★

Neve Campbell is a Canadian film and television star. She was born in Guelph, Ontario on October 3, 1973. Her mother, Marnie, is a yoga instructor and psychologist, and her father, Gerry Campbell, is an immigrant to Canada from Glasgow, Scotland who taught high school drama classes in Mississauga, Ontario. Neve has two younger stepbrothers named Damian and Alex, and an older brother named Christian. Alex and Christian are actors as well. Neve's maternal grandparents ran a theatre company in the Netherlands and her paternal grandparents were also performers.

Neve's parents divorced when she was two years old and she and her brother lived mainly with their father, who had custody of them. They made regular visits to their mother's home. When Neve was six, her father took her to see a ballet called *The Nutcracker* and it was after this event that she decided to take up dancing. She was such a talented dancer that, when she was nine, she was offered a full scholarship and began training with the National Ballet School of Canada. Neve studied six different styles of dancing such as jazz, flamenco, modern, hip hop, and classical ballet. In time, Neve appeared in the productions of the *Nutcracker* and *Sleeping Beauty*.

Neve's original goal was to become a professional ballerina but ballet training takes its toll on the dancer's body and she suffered from a series of injuries, such as shin splints, fallen arches, pulled calf muscles, cracked ribs, bursitis, and tendonitis. The world of professional dancing is often a breeding ground for competition and backstabbing. At the age of 14, Neve suffered a nervous breakdown that caused all of her hair to fall out. All these events convinced her to give up dancing. At 15, Neve moved from dancing to acting and performed in *The Phantom of the Opera* at the Pantages Theatre in Toronto. She was the youngest performer in the cast at that time and she performed in 800 shows.

In 1992, Neve's career took off on Canadian television and she made guest appearances on shows such as *The Kids in the Hall*, *Are You Afraid of the Dark*, and *Kung Fu: The Legend Continues*. In 1994, Neve was cast in the teen drama *Catwalk* and also appeared in three other television movies. She also took the part of Julia Salinger Holbrook in the hit Fox series *Party of Five* and played on it until its final season in 2000. In 1996, Neve appeared in three scary thriller movies, *The Canterville Ghost*, *The Craft*, and *Scream*, which was a box office success. In 1997, she played the same role of Sidney Prescott in *Scream 2* and, with actors Matt Dillon and Kevin Bacon, in *The Wild Things*. In 1998, Neve was featured in the movie *54* and lent her voice to the animated feature *Lion King II: Simba's Pride*.

Neve's next projects were roles in two comedy films, *Three to Tango* (1999) and *Drowning Mona* (2000). These were followed by the dramatic features *Panic* (2000) and *Scream 3*, where she was chased by a psycho again. During the years of 2000-2001, Neve starred in the dramatic productions *Intimate Affairs*, *Last Call*, and *Lost Junction*. In 2003, she produced, wrote and starred in the movie called *The Company*, which told the story of a ballet company. It gave audiences an insight into the world of a ballet dancer and the demands this art form has on a dancer's mind and body.

During 2006, Neve turned her attention to live acting and made her stage debut in a play at the old Vic Theatre in London, England. In 2007, she presented at the United Kingdom rally of Live Earth at Wembley Stadium in London. Today, Neve continues to act in various media and is happily married to English actor John Light. ★

Neve Campbell

Name: _____ Date: _____

Reading Skills

Answer each question with a good sentence.

1. What gave Neve the desire to take up ballet? _____
_____

2. Why do you think Neve has natural acting ability? _____
_____

3. How do you know Neve was a talented ballet dancer? _____
_____

4. How do you know that Neve was a diversified dancer? _____
_____

5. How is ballet dancing a stressful art form? _____
_____

6. Why did Neve choose acting over dancing? _____
_____

7. Which of her movies became a box office success? _____
_____

8. Which movie did Neve write, produce and star in? _____
_____

Vocabulary Skills

A. In the biography, locate the following parts of speech

1. six common nouns: _____
_____
_____

2. six proper nouns: _____
_____
_____

3. six verbs: _____
_____
_____

4. six adjectives: _____
_____
_____

5. six adverbs: _____
_____
_____

B. Match the words in the box to their meanings. Record them on the lines provided.

maternal	flamenco	bursitis
custody	junction	stadium
toll	insight	tendonitis

1. in charge of _____
2. paid a price _____
3. a Spanish gypsy dance _____
4. a place of joining _____
5. a view of the inside _____
6. inflamation of a joint _____
7. a place to watch sports _____
8. soreness in a tendon _____

Intelligent, Talented, Successful ★ Sandra Oh ★

Sandra Oh is an award winning Canadian actress whose Korean name is Mi-Joa Oh. She was born on July 20, 1971 to middle-class Korean immigrant parents Joon-Soo (John) and Young-Nam, who came to Canada in the late 1960s. Her father is a business man and her mother a biochemist. Sandra was raised along with a brother and sister in Nepean, a suburb of Ottawa. She began acting and taking ballet lessons at an early age. At the age of ten, she played the Wizard of Woe in a class musical called *The Canada Goose*.

Sandra attended Sir Robert Borden High School during her teenage years. She was a good student and was involved in many extra-curricular activities. Sandra was an Honour Role Student and involved with the Student's Council. During her senior year, she was voted as "Head Girl" or co-president of the high school. During her final year, she began an Environmental Club called BASE (Borden Active Students for the Environment). She campaigned against the use of Styrofoam cups. Sandra was also an avid participant in volleyball and cross-country skiing.

Sandra knew that her dancing skills were not strong enough for her to become a professional dancer and focused her attention on the development of her acting skills. She was involved in drama classes, acted in school plays, and joined the school drama club. With the drama club, she took part in the Canadian Improv Games and Skit Row High, a comedy group. Sandra was offered a four year scholarship in journalism at Carleton University when she graduated. She rejected the offer and instead decided to study acting at the famous National Theatre School in Montreal, paying for her own way. After graduating in 1993, Sandra starred in a stage production called *Oleanna* in London, Ontario. At the same time, she won roles in biographical films that were about the life stories of two important female Chinese Canadians. In *The Diary of Evelyn Lau*, Sandra portrayed the Vancouver author Evelyn Lau and beat out over 1,000 other actresses who had auditioned for the part. In the second film, Sandra portrayed Adrienne Clarkson in a CBC biopic of Clarkson's life called *Adrienne Clarkson Presents*.

In 1994, Sandra became famous in Canada for her lead performance in the Canadian film *Double Happiness*, and also won the Genie Award for Best Actress. In this movie, Sandra portrays a young Chinese-Canadian woman struggling to live her own life while breaking away from her family's oppressive traditions. In 1996, Sandra moved to Los Angeles to begin the first of seven seasons in the comedy series *Arli$$*, playing the role of Rita Wu, who is an assistant to a sports agent. For her performance in this role, Sandra won the Cable Ace Award for Best Actress in a Comedy. Sandra has appeared in other Canadian films such as *Long Life, Happiness, Prosperity*, and *Last Night*. For her role in *Last Night*, she received her second Best Actress Genie Award in 1999.

In the United States, Sandra is known for her roles in popular films such as *Under the Tuscan Sun*, *Sideways*, and *Dancing at the Blue Iguana*. Sandra is known on American television for her current role in the ABC medical series *Grey's Anatomy*, in which she plays Christina Yang, a young medical intern learning the ropes at Seattle Grace Hospital. In 2006, Sandra won a Golden Globe Award for Best Supporting Actress in a series and, in the same year, a Screen Actors Award in a Drama Series. In 2008, Sandra received her fourth consecutive Emmy nomination for her work on the series.

Sandra has never forgotten her love for stage acting and has appeared in several plays, such as *Dogeaters* and *Stop Kiss* in theatres in New York. In 2008, Sandra was the host for the 28th Genie Awards in Canada. ★

Sandra Oh

Name: _____   Date: _____

Reading Skills

Answer each question with a complete sentence.

1. What leadership qualities did Sandra Oh display while she attended high school?

2. How do you know that Sandra Oh was active athletically during high school?

3. How do you know that Sandra Oh was an intelligent student?

4. How do you know Sandra Oh enjoyed performing at her school?

5. Do you think Sandra's decision to reject the offer of a scholarship was a good one?

6. How do you think her parents felt about her decision to not take the scholarship?

7. Brainstorm and make a list of ten adjectives that could be used to describe Sandra Oh as an actor and as a person.

Vocabulary Skills

A. Interrogative sentences are sentences that ask questions. When punctuating an interrogative sentence, use a question mark.

Pretend that you are interviewing Sandra Oh. On the lines provided, record four good interrogative sentences that you would ask her.

1. _____

2. _____

3. _____

4. _____

B. Declarative sentences are sentences that make statements. They say something about a place, person, thing or idea. When punctuating a declarative sentence, use a period at the end.

On the lines provided write four declarative sentences about Sandra Oh.

1. _____

2. _____

3. _____

4. _____

Strong Advocate of Canadian Culture ★ Wendy Crewson ★

Wendy Crewson dreamed about being an actress when she was a very young girl. She was born on May 9, 1956 in Hamilton, Ontario. Her family moved frequently as her father sold farm equipment. Wendy graduated from high school in Point Claire, Quebec and attended John Abbott College to study theatre arts in Montreal. She then attended Queen's University in Kingston, Ontario, studying drama. While at the university, Wendy won the prestigious Lorne Greene Award for outstanding work in the theatre. From Canada, Wendy journeyed to London, England, to study at the Webber Douglas Academy.

While on vacation in Canada, Wendy auditioned for a part in the CBC TV drama *War Brides* (1980). She got the part and played the role of Terry Lowe, a young woman who works at an aircraft factory, whose husband was killed in the Dieppe Raid in World War II. Wendy won an Actra Award for Best Actress for her performance. During 1985, Wendy appeared in the crime dramas *Night Heat*, *Street Legal*, and *Adderly* on Canadian television. In 1987, Crewson appeared on *Hard Copy* on CBS, where she met her present husband, actor Michael Murphy. They were married in 1988 and lived in New York City, then moved to San Francisco with their two children, and in 2001, returned to live in Toronto permanently.

Crewson appeared in dozens of Canadian television movies in the 1980s. One role that brought her Hollywood attention was in *Getting Married in Buffalo Jump* (1990) where she played Sophie Ware, a young Toronto musician, who returns to her family's ranch in Alberta and falls in love with her hired hand. Her future projects took place on the big screen. These included *The Good Son* (1993), in which Wendy played the mother of a murderous young man, *Corina* (1994) with Whoopi Goldberg and Ray Liotta, *Air Force One* (1997), as the First Lady opposite Harrison Ford as President, *Gang Related* (1997) as a street smart prosecutor, and *Bicentennial Man* (1999) with Robin Williams.

In many films, Wendy felt that she was being typecast as an anxious wife and mother and decided to return to Canada. In Canada's film and television industry, Wendy Crewson has become a hardworking mainstay and an actress that directors and producers can count on. In 1992, Wendy received a Gemini Award nomination for *I'll Never Get to Heaven* in which she plays an Irish Catholic mother who challenges her faith in the church. During 1998, Crewson appeared in the series *Due South* and received a Gemini Award for Best Performance in a Guest Role. In the same year, Crewson had a role as the wife of an astronaut in the American miniseries called *From Earth to Mars,* which told of the stoic bravery shown by the wives of astronauts.

In the movie, called *Sleeping Dogs Lie* (1999), Crewson plays the role of a grieving widow and murder suspect. During the same year, Crewson won a Gemini Award for her superb performance in the right to die drama entitled *At the End of the Day: The Sue Rodriguez Story*. In this film, Wendy portrays a woman afflicted with ALS who bravely struggles to die with dignity. In the film *Hunt for Justice: The Louise Arbour Story,* Cindy portrays a Canadian war-crimes prosecutor and in *The Man who Lost Himself,* she plays the wife of a CFL star who lost his memory after a car crash. Her most recent performance was as the unfeeling director of a nursing home in the feature film *Away From Her.*

Wendy Crewson has had eight Gemini nominations and won four during her acting career. In 2007, Wendy received the ACTRA Award of Excellency. For many years, Wendy has been a strong advocate for Canadian culture and has pushed for more homegrown dramas on television and in Canadian films. ★

Wendy Crewson

Name: _____   Date: _____

Reading Skills

Skim through Wendy Crewson's biography to find out the year and the name of the film in which she played each role.

1. **Role:** a woman on a ranch who falls in love with a hired hand.
   Year: _____ **Film:** _____

2. **Role:** a woman confused about her faith
   Year: _____ **Film:** _____

3. **Role:** the mother of a harmful young man
   Year: _____ **Film:** _____

4. **Role:** wife of an astronaut
   Year: _____ **Film:** _____

5. **Role:** a woman who no longer wants to live
   Year: _____ **Film:** _____

6. **Role:** a woman who is a murder suspect
   Year: _____ **Film:** _____

7. **Role:** the wife of an American president
   Year: _____ **Film:** _____

8. **Role:** a war-crimes prosecutor
   Year: _____ **Film:** _____

9. **Role:** the wife of a car crash victim
   Year: _____ **Film:** _____

10. **Role:** the director of a nursing home
    Year: _____ **Film:** _____

Vocabulary Skills

Complete the crossword puzzle with words found in the biography. Carefully read the puzzle clues.

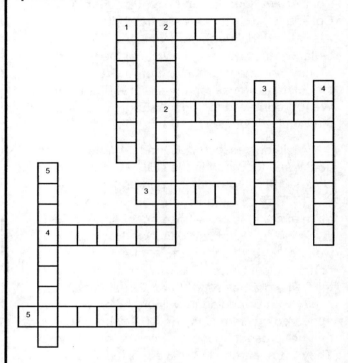

Puzzle Clues:

Down:

1. to believe someone is guilty of wrong doing
2. intended to last a long time
3. type of school
4. to support something publicly
5. able to inflict great harm

Across:

1. grand, majestic, the best
2. to cause pain
3. a person who can hide feelings
4. proud and stately manner
3. the customs and heritage of a people

ISBN: 9781554950898   SSJ1-78 • Female Actors

A Child Star — ★ Anna Paquin ★

Anna Paquin rocketed to stardom when she was an 11 year old child after her impressive performance in the independent film *The Piano*. She is one of the most remarkable talents that Hollywood has ever had. Anna is the youngest child of Brian and Mary Paquin and was born in Winnipeg, Manitoba on July 24, 1982. Her full name is Anna Helene Paquin. Her mother was a native of New Zealand and the family moved there when Anna was four.

Anna received her early education and part of her secondary education in New Zealand. The rest of her high school studies were done in a school in Los Angeles, which she attended when her parents divorced and her mother moved to the United States. During her youth, Anna had many hobbies such as playing the cello, viola, and the piano. She also enjoyed gymnastics, ballet, swimming, and downhill skiing.

As a child, Anna had no intentions of becoming an actress and the only dramatic part she ever played was as a skunk in a school production. It was a wonderful fluke that she became an actress. While attending the audition for the movie *The Piano* with her sister, she caught the eye of the casting directors and was asked to do a reading. They saw something very special in this nine year old and cast her as Flora, the daughter of a mute woman. Over 5,000 other hopefuls had tried out for the part. During the film, Anna delivered a mature and moving performance as Flora, who often speaks for her silent mother. The movie was a box office success and Anna Paquin, at the age of 11, was nominated for a Best Supporting Actress Oscar in 1994. To the surprise of many who attended the Academy Awards, Anna won. She is the second youngest actress to win an Academy Award after Tatum O'Neal in *Paper Moon* in 1973. Anna is the first Canadian-born actress to win a Best Supporting Actress Oscar.

After the movie, Anna and her family didn't plan to have her pursue an acting career. Anna kept receiving offers for new roles but kept refusing them. She did do some commercials and did voice work for an audio book called *The Magnificent Nose* in 1994. In 1996, Anna did accept an offer to play the role of *Jane Eyre* in the movie by the same name. She proved that winning the Oscar was not a fluke and slowly began to build her acting career, only doing interesting characters, instead of high profile projects. During the same year, Anna played the role of a young girl who helps to raise a flock of Canada Geese in the children's drama *Fly Away Home*. While in Canada shooting the film, Anna made five television commericals for a telephone company in her former hometown of Winnipeg.

In 1997, in the film *Amistad*, Anna earned an impressive cameo as Isabella, Queen of Spain. In time, Anna made the transition from a child-actress to a more mature one with her performances in *Hurlyburly* (1998), *A Walk on the Moon* (1999), the popular science fiction film *X-Men* (2000), *Almost Famous* (2000), and *Finding Forrester* (2000).

In 2007, Anna took the role of Elaine Goodale in *Bury My Heart at Wounded Knee* for HBO. She played the role of a real-life poet and Indian Rights Advocate who had married a Sioux doctor, played by another Canadian, Adam Beach. Anna continues to make movies, but has also lent her talent to acting in Off-Broadway plays. ★

Anna Paquin

Name: _____ Date: _____

Reading Skills

Circle the correct answer(s) to each question.

1. In which country was Anna Paquin born?

   New Zealand   Australia   Canada   England

2. How old was Anna when she was discovered?

   fifteen   eleven   nine   thirteen

3. Which musical instruments does Anna play?

   trumpet   cello   guitar   piano
   harp   violin   viola   drums

4. What was the name of her first film?

   Amistad   *X-Men*   *The Piano*   *Hurlyburly*

5. What does the word "mute" mean?

   can't hear   can't see   can't feel   can't talk

6. How many other little girls auditioned for the role of Flora in the movie *The Piano*?

   2,000   1,000   5,000   7,000

7. What reaction was felt when Anna won the Oscar at the Academy Awards?

   anger   jealousy   surprise   disgust

8. What award did Anna receive for her supporting role in *The Piano*?

   Emmy   Medal   Juno   Oscar   Star

9. What did Anna help raise in the film *Fly Away Home*?

   chickens   geese   ducks   birds   swans

10. In which countries did Anna receive her education?

    United States   Canada   New Zealand

Vocabulary Skills

Match each word in the box to its correct meaning

intentions	fluke	impressive
transition	cameo	remarkable
tragedy	befell	

1. to come about; happen; occur
   _____

2. a background role or part
   _____

3. worthy of notice; extraordinary
   _____

4. purposeful; deliberately; intended
   _____

5. an intensely sad event
   _____

6. a piece of good luck
   _____

7. a change of action
   _____

8. exciting emotion or admiration
   _____

Research Skills

Anna Paquin spent most of her childhood in the beautiful country called New Zealand.

Research this country using resources in the library or on the Internet.

Find out five interesting facts about it and record the facts in an interesting paragraph.

Dancer, Actress, Writer ★ Meg Tilly ★

Meg Tilly is a sweet-faced, soft spoken young woman who made a name for herself as an actress in the mid-1980s. She is the opposite of most young actresses and has often shunned the limelight which comes with being a celebrity. Meg was born as Margaret E. Chan on Valentine's Day 1960, in Long Beach California. She is the daughter of Patricia Tilly, a school teacher and former actress, and Harry Chan, a Chinese American car salesman. Meg is the third of four children. Her sister, Jennifer Tilly, is also an actress. Meg's parents divorced when she was three years old and her mother took the children to Texada Island in British Columbia, where they were raised by her and a stepfather.

At the age of 12, Meg began to take dance lessons and became a highly gifted ballerina. When Meg turned 17 she joined the Connecticut Ballet Company, became part of the Throne Dance Theatre Company and toured with it. Her dancing ability, and her connection with the touring company, led to her first film role as one of the many background dancers in the famous dance movie *Fame* (1980). This role opened many doors for her. Unfortunately, her dreams of having a dancing career were dashed when she seriously hurt her back. Meg then turned to acting after her experience in *Fame*.

Meg was frequently typecast as the innocent girl-next-door character. In 1981, Meg was cast in the TV movie entitled *The Trouble With Grandpa* and also appeared in an episode of the series *Hill Street Blues*. Meg also played the role of a kind waitress who unwisely befriends Norman Bates, a man who has just been released from a mental hospital in the film *Psycho II*. In 1982, she appeared with Matt Damon in the heart-warming teen drama *Tex*. Unfortunately, it did not do well at the box office.

Meg's biggest break came in the yuppie classic *The Big Chill* (1983). She played the role of Chloe, the young girlfriend of a dead man, whose seven friends from college have come to his funeral and, later, have a reunion at a very posh South Carolina house. After *The Big Chill*, Meg became popular and gained much attention, with pictures and articles written about her in magazines and newspapers, which she found was an invasion of her privacy and disliked intensely. As a result, she chose to act in two very unflattering roles. The films, *One Dark Night* (1983) and *Impulse* (1984), were trashy science fiction thrillers. During the filming of her next film, *Amadeus*, in which she had the role of the wife of Mozart, Meg tore a ligament in her leg playing soccer with some children and was forced to drop out. In 1986, in the film *Agnes of God*, Meg plays an innocent nun who was accused of murdering her newborn baby. For this role she won the Golden Globe for Best Supporting Actress and was nominated for a Best Supporting Actress Academy Award. During the same year, Meg played a sweet but feisty police officer in the comedy film *Off Beat*.

Meg starred in a thriller called *Masquerade* in 1988, as an orphaned millionairess. This film received good reviews and reaffirmed her abilities as an actress. In the same year, Meg played the role of a mysterious, beautiful woman whose eerie past begins to haunt the young man she marries in the film *Girl on a Swing*. During the next four years, Meg played a wide variety of roles in various movies that were not always winners. Her last acting role was in 1995 in a television movie entitled *Journey*. In the film, Meg plays a mother who abandons her two children and leaves them in the care of grandparents. Since then, Meg has left acting to focus on her personal life and to use her creative skills in writing. She has written two books called *Singing Songs* and *Gemma*. ★

Meg Tilly

Name: _____ Date: _____

Reading Skills

Read each statement carefully. Underline all the true statements about Meg Tilly.

1. Meg Tilly is a tall, blonde, beautiful woman who modelled before she became an actress.
2. Jennifer Tilly is a well known actress and is Meg's sister.
3. Meg was born on Christmas Day on Texada Island in British Columbia.
4. Meg began taking ballet lessons at the age of five.
5. Meg's dancing career ended when she hurt her back.
6. Meg was the dancing star in the movie called *Fame*.
7. When Meg could no longer dance, she decided to become an actress.
8. Some of Meg's movies did not do well at the box office.
9. Meg's break came when she played the role of a waitress in the film *Psycho II*.
10. Meg loves to act, but does not like the attention she receives from the media.
11. Meg Tilly has played a wide variety of roles.
12. Unfortunately, Meg's acting talent has never been honoured with any awards.

Vocabulary Skills

A. Classify each group of words as antonyms (A), synonyms (S) or homonyms (H). Record the correct letter on the line provided.

1. divorced, married _____
2. gifted, talented _____
3. toured, travelled _____
4. role, roll _____
5. dashed, destroyed _____
6. seldom, frequently _____
7. episode, chapter _____
8. night, knight _____
9. beat, beet _____
10. losers, winners _____

B. On the line provided, write the base word for each of the following words.

1. intensely _____
2. thrillers _____
3. unflattering _____
4. unfortunately _____
5. seriously _____
6. unwisely _____
7. millionairess _____
8. mysterious _____
9. trashy _____
10. reunion _____

Ontario's Famous Five ★ The Barenaked Ladies ★

For over a decade, a band called the Barenaked Ladies, or BNL, has been the pride of Canada, achieving great success at home, across the border, and abroad. The band's funny and very unconventional style, and its members ability to get away with singing about whatever they please, has made the Barenaked Ladies famous. The members of the band are Jim Creeggan, Kevin Hearn, Steven Page, Ed Robertson, Tyler Stewart and former band member Andy Creeggan.

In the beginning, the band began with the duo of Ed Robertson and Steven Page. Both attended the same schools in Scarborough, Ontario but were not friends until they met at a Harvey's restaurant after a concert when they were teenagers. During their conversation they found out they shared many of the same interests and they became good friends. Their friendship grew stronger when Ed and Steven were counsellors at a music camp, where they played songs together, and Steven discovered Ed's ability to harmonize. Both teens attended a Bob Dylan concert together which they found boring so they began to amuse themselves by critiquing the show and making up names for various bands. Out of this brainstorming exercise came the name "Barenaked Ladies," which they both have had to defend on several occasions during the band's career.

The Barenaked Ladies' first performance took place when Robertson needed Page to help him play at a benefit because his former band had just broken up. Neither musician had been able to attend any rehearsals and as a result they played every song they both knew and improvised during the show. This element of improvised raps, songs and banter are still part of each BNL concert.

One night, while performing in Toronto, Page and Robertson invited friends Andy Creeggan, a percussionist, and Jim Creeggan, a bassist, whom they had met at music camp, to play with them at a Christmas club show. The brothers soon became part of the band. Six months later, Andy Creeggan went to Ecuador on a student exchange trip, leaving the band without a percussionist. During the summer of 1990, at a Busker's festival, the members met drummer Tyler Stewart, who took over Andy's job. When Andy returned, he found out he had been replaced and was disappointed at first, but moved on to play keyboards for the band. During 1991, the band set out on their first full tour of Canada and also recorded their first song, "Yellow Tape." A copy of the recording was sent to all the labels in Canada and was rejected by everyone. The band began selling them off the stage and before long, people began asking for the tape in local stores. Sales of the tape grew, making it the first independent (Indie) rock release to achieve platinum status in Canada.

BNL released its first full album, "Gordon," in 1992 and it was a big success in Canada. In 1994, BNL's second album, "Maybe You Should Drive," didn't do as well and the tour they made to the United States failed miserably. It was then that Andy Creeggan decided to leave the band as he was disappointed with the band's direction and was not comfortable with its reputation as well. At the same time, some of the other band members were unhappy with each other and not speaking. In order to save the band from falling apart, the members signed with Terry McBride and Nettwork as their management with whom they are still working today.

In 1997, Tyler Stewart invited his friend Kevin Hearn to replace Andy Creeggan as keyboardist for their new tour. In 1998, the band released an album called "Stunt," which became their greatest success and break through into the United States. Just after this great achievment, Kevin Hearn was diagnosed with leukemia, had to have a bone marrow transplant and spent several months at a Toronto hospital recovering. Two of his friends covered for him until he could rejoin the band.

The Barenaked Ladies have continued to produce many more albums and singles in 2008, including "Snacktime" which is a collection of original children's songs. They have received numerous nominations and won four Junos in 1993. These talented band members still have much more to offer to their fans and will be heard from in the future. ★

The Barenaked Ladies

Name: _____   Date: _____

Reading Skills

Complete the sentences with the names of BNL band members.

1. _____ was diagnosed with leukemia in 1998 and spent several months in the hospital.

2. _____ and _____ were percussionists for the BNL band.

3. _____ and _____ were counsellors at a music camp in Scarborough.

4. _____ left the band to go on a student exchange trip to Ecuador.

5. _____ and _____ formed and named the BNL band.

6. Feeling disappointed and unhappy, _____ left the BNL band after their United States tour in 1994.

7. _____'s ability to harmonize was a useful skill.

8. _____ and his brother Andy were invited to play with the BNL band at a Christmas show.

9. _____ met the members of the BNL band at a Busker's festival.

10. Ed Robertson needed _____ to help him play at a benefit when his band broke up.

11. _____ and _____ met at a Harvey's restaurant after a concert.

12. _____ invited his friend _____ to take Andy's place as the band's keyboardist.

Vocabulary Skills

A. Look up the following words in the dictionary and record their meanings on the lines provided.

1. banter: _____
2. improvised: _____
3. reputation: _____
4. decade: _____
5. duo _____
6. harmonize: _____

B. Write the root word for each of the following on the line provided.

1. unconventional: _____
2. harmonize: _____
3. conversation: _____
4. performance: _____
5. rehearsals: _____
6. miserably: _____
7. collection: _____
8. nominations: _____

Research Skills

Locate a map of the world to find the country of Ecuador. In which continent is it located?

_____

Alberta's Musical Prince ★ Kalan Porter ★

Kalan Porter was the second winner of the reality television series Canadian Idol. He was born on November 11, 1985 and raised near a town called Irvine in Alberta. Kalan grew up on a buffalo and cattle ranch and often had to participate in various ranching chores such as weaning calves, feeding, corralling and branding cattle. He is the oldest of three children.

Kalan's musical ability began when he was very young. His mother claims he could hum parts of a lullaby at 18 months. Kalan's classical music training began at the age of eight with the violin and the viola. He also plays other instruments such as the bass, guitar, and piano and began vocal lessons at the age of ten. As a child, Kalan participated in many local and provincial music competitions and has received numerous awards for vocal, violin, musical theatre, viola, and Chamber Ensemble.

At the age of 16, Kalan joined the family band called SWASS, made up of seven members. The band plays a variety of music genre such as rock, sacred, country and Celtic. It has performed at trade shows, conventions, Canada Day celebrations, and charity fund raisers. SWASS also won first place during the Battle of the Bands in Alberta. Kalan also played classical music with various ensembles and an orchestra.

Kalan's friends describe him as intelligent, genuine, family-oriented and passionate about his music. He is good with children as a teacher and mentor. His favourite foods are sushi and steak. Kalan loves to wakeboard, snowboard and play volleyball. His friends claim that he is willing to participate in just about any activity and has white water rafted, scuba dived and sky dived. In 2004, his family encouraged him to audition for Canadian Idol when the auditions came to Edmonton. Kalan appeared as a very young and nervous teenager during his audition but he surprised

and wowed the judges with his rendition of the song "House of the Rising Sun." From the very beginning, the judges predicted that he would win the whole thing.

During the competition, Kalan used his natural talent, years of training, hard work and charm to out maneuver all the other contestants. On September 16, 2004, in front of a live TV audience and millions of viewers, Kalan was crowned Canadian Idol. He immediately signed a recording contract with Sony/BMG Music Canada. The next day his single "Awake in a Dream" was released. The ballad went on to become eight times platinum and remained on the top of Canada's single charts for over three months. It was the biggest-selling single debut ever for a Canadian artist.

In November of 2004, Kalan's full-length CD "219 Days" was released and went double platinum, which was an amazing feat for a Canadian artist.

In 2005, Kalan went on to compete in World Idol 2 against Ruben Studdard and all the other winners from other countries' second idol shows. In the same year, his album "219" Days" was nominated for two Juno Awards. Kalan's musical talent and training and his positive attitude will undoubtedly lead to even greater success in the music industry in the years to come. ★

Kalan Porter

Name: _____   Date: _____

Reading Skills | Vocabulary Skills

Locate a sentence, in the biography, that proves each statement below is true. Record the first five words of the sentence on the line provided.

1. Kalan Porter comes from an agricultural area in Alberta.
   _____

2. Kalan's family had their own band.
   _____

3. The SWASS band was successful and talented.
   _____

4. Kalan's talent was noticed when he was quite young.
   _____

5. He impressed the judges of Canadian Idol during his audition.
   _____

6. Kalan's personality and musical talent brought him success.
   _____

7. His first single "Awake in a Dream" was a successful recording.
   _____

8. **Circle the words that describe Kalan.**

   intelligent   passionate   grumpy   vain

   caring   genuine   obnoxious   rude

   self-centred   thoughtless   adventurous

   carefree   talented   selfish   careless

A. Use the dictionary to help you divide the following words into syllables using a slash (/).

1. reality   5. intelligent
2. Alberta   6. passionate
3. corralling   7. audition
4. provincial   8. competition

B. Locate four compound words in the biography. Record them on the lines provided.

1. _____
2. _____
3. _____
4. _____

C. Match the word from the biography to its meaning with a line.

1. genuine •   • a wise and trusted advisor

2. mentor •   • interpretation of the meaning

3. predicted •   • an instrument shaped like a violin

4. viola •   • high quality music

5. classical •   • a group of musicians used in a performance

6. ensemble •   • forecast

7. rendition •   • real, true, sincere

Canada's Musical Ambassador ★ Bryan Adams ★

During the mid 1980's to the mid 1990's, Bryan Adams was one of the most successful Canadian singers, songwriters, guitarists, and recording artists in popular music worldwide. Dressed in blue jeans, sneakers and white T-shirts, Adams performed and sang his own pop/rock songs and ballads to audiences numbering in the tens of thousands all over the world.

Bryan was born on November 5, 1959 in Kingston, Ontario to English parents. His father was a military diplomat and his occupation caused the family to move extensively during Bryan's childhood. They lived in England, Israel, France, Portugal, and Austria during the 1960s. When his parents separated during the 1970s, Bryan, his brother, and his mother returned to Ottawa and then settled in Vancouver, British Columbia.

During 1973, Bryan dropped out of high school at the age of 15 to audition for rock bands as a lead singer. At the age of 16, he was performing with bands such as Shock and Sweeney Todd in nightclubs. In 1978, Bryan met Jim Vallance in a Vancouver music store. Vallence was looking for a singer while Adams was looking for a route to a musical career. The two musicians began writing together and recording demo tapes, which they sent to recording companies. A&M Records liked what they heard and signed Bryan to a contract.

In 1980, Bryan recorded his first solo song "Let Me Take You Dancing." He was not happy with the recording as the record company sped up his voice and changed the background to a disco beat. It sold many copies and was played in discos all over the world. His first album entitled "Bryan Adams" was recorded and released in the same year and although it was not a best seller, it did launch a long songwriting partnership between Adams and Vallance. Bryan's second album, "You Want It, You Got It," was recorded in New York and he began playing in small clubs and arenas to promote it. The media began to notice this rising rock star. His third album, "Cuts Like a Knife," did very well and he began touring the world with the very popular band Journey. Bryan's fourth album "Reckless" had six top singles and his song "Heaven" became the most popular song in

the United States, and was also used in a movie in 1984. The album was also certified five times platinum and, in the music world, Bryan Adams was now considered a superstar.

During his busy career, Bryan has been nominated for many different awards and has won 16 Junos and 3 Grammys as well as numerous honours from other countries. He has recorded 14 albums, 30 hit singles, and has sold over 60 million albums all over the world. He has been inducted into Canada's Walk of Fame and the Canadian Music Hall of Fame.

Bryan Adams has been recognized as a social activist participating in concerts and other activities to help raise money and awareness for Amnesty International, food for starving people in South Africa, the freeing of political prisoner Nelson Mandela, Cancer, and the saving of endangered animals. He continues to perform at sellout concerts and to make new music. He has become one of the most popular singers and songwriters in the world and Canadians are very proud of his accomplishments. ★

Bryan Adams

Name: _____ Date: _____

Reading Skills

Circle each true statement about Bryan Adams.

1. Bryan Adams has never won a Grammy for his singing or his music.
2. Bryan's father was a military diplomat and the family lived in different countries.
3. While performing at his concerts, Bryan usually dresses in black.
4. Shock and Sweeney Todd were the first bands that had Bryan Adams for a lead singer.
5. Bryan dropped out of school at the age of 15 to pursue a career in music.
6. Jim Vallance and Bryan Adams played in the same band together.
7. Bryan Adams has participated in many concerts to raise money for people in need and for various other causes.
8. Adams was considered a superstar after his album "Reckless" went platinum five times.
9. His first album, called "Bryan Adams," was very successful in Canada and the United States.
10. Bryan Adams has become a very famous Canadian throughout the world.
11. Bryan Adams was born on November 17, 1959 in Kingston, Ontario.
12. Adams has been inducted into the Canadian Music Hall of Fame and Canada's Walk of Fame.

Vocabulary Skills

A. Skim through the biography to find examples of the following parts of speech. Record five words in each box.

Adjectives

Verbs

Singular Nouns

Plural Nouns

Proper Nouns

Prepositions

Research Skills:

Using a large wall map or an atlas, locate the countries named in the biography. Record their names on the lines provided in the correct alphabetical order.

_____
_____
_____
_____
_____

Four Mississauga Lads ★ Billy Talent ★

Billy Talent is a Canadian rock band that began in 1993 in Mississauga, Ontario. Its members are Benjamin Kowalewicz (vocals), Ian D'Sa (guitar, vocals), Jon Gallant (bass, vocals), and Aaron Solowoniuk (drums, percussion). Their sound is original and unique as they did not emulate popular bands when they began playing together.

In the beginning, Ben and Jon belonged to a local band called To Each His Own. Ben played drums and Jon played bass. Aaron Solowoniuk joined the group later to play drums, while Ben moved on to do the vocals. During a talent show held at their high school, the group met Ian D'Sa who played in another band called Dragonflower. The two bands began playing together at local pool halls and bars. Eventually, both bands were merged into one called The Other One for a short time, and eventually came to be called Pezz.

The group began writing and performing their own songs and gained recognition in their local area as well as in the wider Toronto indie music scene. Their first demo, recorded in Ian D'Sa's basement in 1994, Was named Demoluca after a friend of the band. In 1995, the band members put all their money together to record a better quality demo called Dudebox. These recordings and continued performances gained a fan base for Pezz in Mississauga and surrounding areas.

After high school, the band members went off to work or to places of higher learning. D'Sa studied animation at Sheridan College; Gallant worked on a business degree; Kowalewicz worked at a radio station, and Solowoniuk got his auto body certificate and worked at Chrysler Canada. During their busy schedule, the band members found the time and the money to record their first full length album in 1998 called Watoosh!

In 2001, the band had to change its name as they were threatened with a lawsuit from an American band with the same name. During that year, Billy Talent became the group's new name, which was inspired by a guitarist with the same name.

One day, Ben happened to run into a co-worker from the radio station 102.1 the edge. He asked her

to come to a club and check out their performance. This paid off for the group as this co-worker was hired by Warner Music Canada in A & R. This connection got them a demo deal with the label. In the fall of 2003, the band released their first full-length, self-titled album "Billy Talent." The recording had successful sales and several good singles. The band played to sold-out shows in Canada and the United States and experienced some success in Europe as well.

In 2004, Billy Talent won a Juno Award for Best New Group of the Year. In 2005 and 2006, the band won Junos for Group of the Year and Best Album of the Year. In 2008, Billy Talent won a Juno for Music DVD of the Year. The group has also been honoured with many MuchMusic Awards, Echo Awards and CASPY Awards.

On March 17, 2006, Aaron Solowoniuk revealed in a personal letter to fans that he was the friend with Multiple Sclerosis in their song "This Is How It Goes." In 1999, Aaron was diagnosed with the disease, which could cause numbness in his limbs, leading to paralysis or loss of vision. At first, Aaron struggled with the reality of the disease but when the medication prescribed by his doctor allowed him to continue drumming with the band, he was able to establish a healthy and positive attitude.

Billy Talent continues to tour Canada and other countries in the world and plans to record more albums. Their popularity has steadily climbed throughout the years. ★

Billy Talent

Name: _____ Date: _____

Reading Skills

Complete each sentence using the words from the biography.

1. The _____ of the Billy Talent _____ came from _____ _____, Ontario.

2. Ian D'Sa plays _____ and was a former member of the band called _____ _____.

3. Aaron _____ developed a _____ called _____ _____ in 1999.

4. _____ Kowalewicz worked at a local _____ _____ after he finished high school.

5. In 2001, the band's name _____ was changed to _____ _____.

6. The band members _____ all of their _____ to record a better _____ called _____.

7. The band won _____ for _____ _____ of the Year and Best _____ of the Year in 2005 and 2006.

8. The Billy Talent band is very proud of their _____ and _____ music.

9. In 2003, the band _____ their first full _____ album called Billy Talent _____ by Warner Music Canada.

Vocabulary Skills

A. Using a dictionary, locate the meaning of the following words. Record each meaning on the line provided.

1. unique: _____
2. merged: _____
3. emulate: _____
4. animation: _____

B. Skim through the biography to find words that are opposite in meaning to the following words. Record each word on the line provided.

1. lower _____
2. empty _____
3. same _____
4. failure _____

C. Skim through the biography to find words that are synonyms to the following words. Record each one on the line provided.

1. noise _____
2. write _____
3. started _____
4. joined _____

Research Skills

Using the Internet, visit a website that can give you information on the disease Multiple Sclerosis. Find out the symptoms and the effects of the disease.

A Modest, Talented Musician ★ Sam Roberts ★

Sam Roberts is a young, rising rock star who is receiving a great deal of attention from various radio stations across Canada. His lyrics are sincere and honest and his sound is rich and rocking. It is the type of music that makes you want to move.

Sam was born on October 2, 1974 in Point-Claire, Quebec to South African parents. At the age of four, he heard a stirring version of "O Canada" being played on a violin and fell in love with the instrument. He told his parents about his desire to learn how to play one and they went out to buy Sam a violin. He took violin lessons until he was 20. Although Sam loved the violin he only played it when he was alone in his room. At the age of 10, Sam got a guitar and he plays it well beyond his bedroom today. At 15, Sam was writing his own songs and creating his own sound. His school years were spent at Loyola High School and McGill University in Montreal.

In 1993, Sam formed a band called William which was later changed to Northstar in 1996. The band's music was played a fair bit on college radio stations, was a MuchMusic feature, and worked around Los Angeles while doing demos. Unfortunately, the band was not successful and was disbanded in 1998.

After the band disbanded, Sam recorded a full length independent debut CD called "Brother Down" at home. He performed all the vocals and instrumental parts himself. In 2001, Sam recorded and released a six song E.P., called "The Inhuman Condition" at Maple Music Recordings. The E.P. sold slowly at first, but by the summer of 2002, his first single "Brother Down" became one of the biggest Canadian hits of the year. Another single, "Don't Walk Away Eileen," quickly followed suit.

In 2003, Sam signed with Universal Music and recorded his full length major label debut

recording "We Were Born in Flame." Two of the singles on the recording were very successful. Sam's band consists of Eric Fares (keyboards, guitar, vocals), Dave Nugent (guitar, vocals), James Hall (bass), and Josh Trager (drums).

In 2006, Sam and his band's new album called "Chemical City" was released in Canada and the United States and shot to number one on Canadian rock radio stations. Three of the songs on this recording were top hit singles.

Sam and his fellow musicians have been very successful over a short period of time and their music and talent have been honoured with various awards. In 2003, they won Junos for Single of the Year, Rock Album of the Year, Artist of the Year and Best Director. In 2007, they won Junos for Video of the Year and Rock Album of the Year.

Sam is bilingual and is able to speak English and French fluently. He married his high school sweetheart Jen of 13 years and they had a baby girl, named Miriam Rose, in January of 2007.

Sam's fans and Canada can expect to see and hear more from him and his music in the future whether it be on the road, on the airwaves or on the move. ★

Sam Roberts

Name: _____   Date: _____

Reading Skills

The statements below may be facts or opinions. On the line beside each one, record the word *Fact* or the word *Opinion*.

1. Canadians can always expect to hear fine music from Sam Roberts. _____

2. Sam grew up and went to school in the province of Quebec. _____

3. Sam's first band had to disband because they did not play well together. _____

4. Sam played his violin in his bedroom because he didn't want anyone to hear him. _____

5. Sam began writing his own songs as a teenager. _____

6. Sam recorded his first independent CD at home, sang all the parts and played all the instruments. _____

7. Sam Roberts will always have a successful career as a rock musician. _____

8. Sam's parents came to Canada from another country. _____

9. Sam Roberts' ability to sing in two languages makes him a better singer. _____

10. Everyone loves to listen to the music played by Sam Roberts and his band. _____

Vocabulary Skills

A. Are the pairs of words antonyms, synonyms or homonyms? Record A for antonyms, S for synonyms, and H for homonyms on the line provided beside each pair of words

1. young, old ___   8. present, future ___
2. type, kind ___   9. here, hear ___
3. south, north ___   10. desires, wishes ___
4. fair, fare ___   11. top, bottom ___
5. learn, teach ___   12. heard, herd ___
6. buy, by ___   13. rode, road ___
7. full, empty ___   14. long, short ___

B. Use each pair of homonyms in good sentences to show their meanings.

1. fair: _____

   fare: _____

2. buy: _____

   by: _____

3. hear: _____

   here: _____

4. heard: _____

   herd: _____

Hamilton's Humble Hero ★ Brian Melo ★

Brian Melo was the fifth winner of Canada's popular television talent contest called Canadian Idol. He is now living a lifelong dream that will enable him to pursue his career as a songwriter and performer.

Brian was born on August 15, 1982 in Hamilton, Ontario to Maria and Augusto Milo, immigrants from Portugal. He is the youngest of four brothers and has one sister. His experiences growing up in a Portuguese family immersed him in song and dance. As a young boy, he enjoyed singing with his family around campfires and remembers being involved with his brother's wedding band playing a tambourine.

While his friends were out getting into trouble, Brian and his best friend spent time chatting on the telephone or sitting around making up silly song lyrics and melodies. During high school, Brian was quite shy and quiet and seldom told his parents about his involvement with various school activities. His parents were not even aware that he sang in a class choir. While in high school, Brian chose his destiny without realizing he had done so. He decided to register for a vocal class because he thought it would be an easy way to earn a credit. During this class, he met a teacher who would change the direction of his life forever.

Linda Gatto was Brian's vocal teacher. She immediately recognized Brian's talent and worked wonders to build his confidence in his singing ability. Gatto gave Brian solos, leads, and more difficult pieces to sing. Her class became the school choir that year and she arranged to have some of her students sing back up vocals for Shania Twain at Copps Coliseum in Hamilton. The cheering of thousands of fans stimulated Brian's desires and dreams of a musical career.

Shortly after this performance, Brian picked up a guitar and learned how to play it. His approach to music became much more serious and he began to write better songs. After high school, Brian worked as a construction worker during the day and sang with a band called Stoked as the lead vocalist in the evenings. The band taught Brian stage presence and movement, and his vocal stamina steadily improved.

When the auditions for Canadian Idol rolled into Toronto, Brian's brother and a friend convinced him to try out. Brian hadn't even thought about auditioning for Canadian Idol because he'd tried out in 2002 and only made it to the first round. This time, he was successful and won the competition. During one of the shows, the judges praised him for his emotional performances and his command of the stage.

Brian signed a contract with Shane Carter and Neil Foster, co-presidents of Sony BMG Music, Canada. On September 13, 2007, his first single, "All I Ever Wanted," was released. After the competition, work began on preparing songs for his debut album. Brian was able to participate in the writer's camps alongside some of Canada's elite music composers and lyricists. His songwriting ability shone through and his fear of not being accepted by this famous group disappeared. On the album, Brian was listed as the co-writer on four of the songs. On November 27, 2007, his debut album called "Livin' It" was released. It contains 12 song tracks that showcase his powerful, distinctive voice and songwriting skills.

The pinnacle of Brian's journey as Canadian Idol was performing for his fans. After winning Canadian Idol, Melo stated, "Now I know I can do anything I set my mind to" and he probably will achieve great fame and success in the music industry. ★

Brian Melo

Name: _____ Date: _____

Reading Skills

Complete each sentence with the correct words from Brian Melo's biography.

1. Brian Melo competed and won the __ _____ Canadian Idol _____ contest.

2. Linda Gatto worked hard to build Brian's _____ in his singing _____.

3. Brian was _____ for his _____ _____ performances and the way he used the _____ by the judges.

4. Brian's parents were _____ from the country of _____ and live in _____ today.

5. Brian was a very _____ teenager and often kept _____ from his _____.

6. During the _____ at Copps Coliseum, Brian was _____ by the _____ of so many fans.

7. When Brian finished school he became a _____ worker during the day and a _____ with a _____ at night.

8. The _____ and the _____ gave Brian Melo a standing _____ for his performance during one of the shows.

9. Brian worked with several famous music _____ and _____ at writers' camps preparing songs for his _____ album.

10. Brian wanted to perform live for all the people who had _____ and _____ him during the _____.

Vocabulary Skills

A. Using a dictionary, find out the meaning of the following words. Record each one on the line provided near the word.

1. pinnacle: _____
2. motivated: _____
3. presence: _____
4. stamina: _____
5. stimulated: _____
6. immersed: _____
7. command: _____
8. distinctive: _____

B. Copy each sentence and put in the missing capitalization and punctuation.

1. mr and mrs mellow your son may very well be the next canadian idol exclaimed zack werner excitedly

   _____
   _____
   _____
   _____
   _____

2. i give every ounce of my heart and soul that i have to my loyal fans who have supported me throughout the idol competition replied brian melo during an interview

   _____
   _____
   _____
   _____
   _____
   _____
   _____

The Punk Rocker Trio

★ Sum 41 ★

Sum 41 is a Canadian rock band that began in Ajax, Ontario. Its current members are Deryck Whibley (lead vocalist, guitarist, keyboardist), Jason McCaslin (bass guitarist, backing vocalist), and Steve Jocz (drums). Other members have come and gone on to play with other bands. In 1999, the group signed an international record deal with Island Records. Their music has been labelled by various critics as pop punk, punk rock, and even skate punk. Today, critics consider Sum 41 as an alternative rock band. The band's later music became known for their politically-driven lyrics.

Sum 41 has released five studio albums, one live album, two live DVDs and more than 15 singles. They have sold over ten million albums worldwide. Since 2006, the band has performed more than 300 times and has become famous for their long and global tours that often last for longer than a year.

Sum 41 has also been involved with the charity group War Child Canada. In 2004, the group helped in the making of a documentary covering the effects of war in the Democratic Republic of the Congo. During the filming, fighting and gunfire broke out all around them and the crew and the band barely escaped unharmed. A United Nations' peacekeeper, Chuck Pelletier, called for armoured carriers to take people out of the hot zone and to safety. The band named their next album "Chuck" to honour Pelletier for helping them. This album went Platinum in Canada and Gold in the United States. The documentary called, "War Child," was released on DVD in 2005 in Canada and the United States.

The members of Sum 41 began their music careers in rival bands during high school. Deryck Jason Whibley was born on March 21, 1980 in Scarborough, Ontario. He was raised by his single teenage mother Michelle Whibley. At the age of 12, Deryck and his mother moved to Ajax, Ontario. During high school, Deryck was involved with several bands before he met Steve Joez. Deryck and Steve became good friends and began a band called Kaspir. Later the name was changed to Sum 41 for a supernova show. Jason McCaslin joined the group in 1999.

Deryck has also developed a strong professional career in the music industry as a producer and manager. In January 2004, Deryck began dating Avril Lavigne, who is also a Canadian rocker. They became engaged on June 27, 2005 during a trip to Venice, Italy. Deryck and Avril were married in a traditional Catholic ceremony on July 15, 2006 at a private estate in Montecito, California. They currently live in Bel Air, Los Angeles, California

Jason Paul McCaslan was born on September 3, 1980 in Toronto, Ontario. Jason began playing bass at the age of 14 and belonged to a grunge garage band called Second Opinion. Jason was given the nickname "Cone" by Deryck Whibley in high school because he often ate ice cream cones at lunch. Unfortunately, Jason no longer eats ice cream as he has become lactose intolerant. Although he seems to be the quietest member, he is the most visible of the band members to its fans, often speaking to the public and answering questions on the band's official website.

Steve Jocz was born on July 23, 1981 in Ajax, Ontario. He attended high school in Ajax along with Jason and Deryck. Steve has the nickname Stevo 32 and is the youngest member of the band. He is also considered the most fun loving member. Steve has an older sister named Jen. They were raised by religious, conservative parents. Steve does not share the same beliefs and political views of his parents. He has adopted a vegan diet in his lifestyle and lives in an apartment in Toronto.

Sum 41 continues to make music, and tours throughout the world, making their fans happy. ☆

Sum 41

Name: _____ Date: _____

Reading Skills

Use the biography to find out the following about the band Sum 41.

1. Where did the members of Sum 41 meet?. _____

2. How many members are in the band? _____

3. Why did Sum 41 go to the Congo in 2004? _____

4. Where did the three members of Sum 41 grow up?_____

5. Who helped the band escape from danger in the Congo?. _____

6. Who are the members of Sum 41? _____ _____

7. Which member of Sum 41 married another famous Canadian rocker?. _____

8. How did Jason McCaslin get his nickname of "Cone?" _____

9. Which member of Sum 41 does not eat meat?_____

10. How many Sum 41 albums have sold so far in their career? _____

11. How many performances has the band given since 2006? _____

12. Which band member is nicknamed Stevo 32? _____

Vocabulary Skills

A. Locate the compound word in the biography that matches each of the following meanings.

1. Someone who works for the United Nations _____

2. A funny name given to a person _____

3. In every country _____

4. A way to live _____

5. Years between the age of 12 and 19 _____

6. Located on the Internet _____

7. All the way through _____

8. The use of weapons that shoot _____

B. Underline the root word in each of the following words.

1. documentary
2. unharmed
3. labelled
4. international
5. global
6. apartment
7. producer
8. currently

Research Skills

Using the Internet find out what each of the following means.

a) lactose intolerant _____

b) vegan _____

A Complicated Girl ☆ Avril Lavigne ☆

Avril Ramona Lavigne is a world famous Canadian singer and songwriter who is also well known for her "skater punk" persona. She rose to fame at the age of 18 with her single called "Complicated", in the spring of 2002. It scaled the charts across the continent and by the summer, the track had reached the top spot among Canadian singles. The popularity of "Complicated" paved the way for the success of Avril's first full-length CD, "Let Go".

Avril was born in Belleville, Ontario on September 27, 1984 to devout Christian parents of French-Canadian descent. When Avril was five years old, her parents moved to a small nearby town called Napanee and it is here where she grew up and attended church and school. At the age of two, Avril's ability to sing was noticed by her mother during church services when she sang the hymns along with her and the congregation.

During her early years, she sang in the local church choir and at the age of ten she began singing country music in competitions at local fairgrounds. Three years later, her vocal talent won her the grand prize in a radio station contest which was a trip to Ottawa to perform a duet in a concert with another famous Canadian country music star, Shania Twain.

By the time Avril reached high school, she began sending videotapes of her stage performances to labels and management companies throughout North America. She was discovered by her first professional manager while singing at a Chapters bookstore in Kingston, Ontario. By the age of sixteen, she was signed by Arista Records which arranged for her to fly to New York City to meet other songwriters and begin working on a demo tape. The representatives of Arista Records were so impressed with her voice, they immediately signed Avril to a contract at the age of sixteen.

Avril briefly returned to Canada, collected her belongings and then returned to Manhattan to begin her professional career, accompanied by her older brother Matt as an escort. Avril has always approached life with an independent attitude of always doing her own thing and when she discovered she was signed to Arista as strictly a vocalist, she refused to sing songs written by someone else. She insisted on having a hand in the writing process. Avril and the New York songwriters did not work well together, so she left New York and went to Los Angeles. It was here on the West Coast that she met producer and songwriter Cliff Magness and developed a good working rapport. Together they worked on Avril's debut album.

In 2002, Avril was named "Best New Artist at the MTV Video Music Awards and at the 2003 Juno Awards she had six nominations and won four Junos. She has also been nominated for eight Grammy Awards but has not won any to date. In February 2004, Avril begin dating fellow Canadian singer Deryck Whibley, the lead singer/guitarist of the pop punk band Sum 41. On June 27, 2005, Deryck proposed to Avril during a gondola ride in Venice and they were married at a private estate in California on July 15, 2006

Avril exhibits musical skills that are far greater than many of her peers. She writes her own songs, plays guitar exceptionally well and her voice displays a very versatile style and range. She is truly a rare talent and a complicated young woman. ☆

Avril Lavigne

Name: _____ Date: _____

Reading Skills

Underline the correct answer and complete each sentence.

1. Avril Lavigne was born in _____.

   (Ottawa, Napanee, Belleville)

2. Her mother noticed Avril's singing ability at the age of _____.

   (seven, nine, two)

3. At the age of ten Avril performed in concert with _____.

   (Celine Dion, Terri Clark, Shania Twain)

4. Avril's hit single was called _____.

   (Sk8ter Boi, When You're Gone, Complicated)

5. Avril was discovered by Arista Records during a performance at a _____.

   (fairground, Chapters' bookstore, concert)

6. Avril signed her first contract with Artista Records at the age of _____.

   (sixteen, nineteen, seventeen)

7. Deryck Whibley proposed to Avril during a _____.

   (gondala ride, bus trip, concert)

8. In the year 2003, Avril won _____.

   (six Junos, five Junos, four Junos)

Vocabulary Skills

Find words in the biography that match the following meanings. Record them on the lines provided.

1. difficult to understand
   _____

2. to climb to the top
   _____

3. to accompany and protect someone
   _____

4. able to get along
   _____

5. an equal in the same profession or social rank
   _____

Divide the following words into syllables. For example: *per - form*.

6. continent _____

7. professional _____

8. management _____

Search for five compound words in the biography. Record them on the lines below.

9. _____
   _____
   _____
   _____
   _____

76

A Diverse Musician

★ Nellie Furtado ★

Nellie was born in Victoria, British Columbia on December 2, 1978 to proud Portuguese parents who named her Nellie Kim Furtado after the Russian gymnast Nellie Kim. Her strong Portuguese cultural background, her interest in different cultures, and her experimentation with different instruments bring a wide variety of sounds to her music.

As a child, Nellie began performing and singing in Portuguese and sang a duet with her mother at church on Portugal Day. She began playing the trombone and ukulele at the age of nine and later mastered the guitar and keyboards. When Nellie was 12, she began writing her own songs and as a teenager played in a Portuguese marching band. During her teenage years she loved to listen to R & B, hip hop, trip hop, Portuguese fado, Brazilian bossa nova and Indian music. Nellie claims that she gets her strong work ethics from her parents as she spent eight summers working as a chambermaid with her mother.

After grade 11, Nellie spent the summer in Toronto and the first musicians she interacted with were rappers and DJs. During her visit, she met Tallis Newkirk, a member of the hip hop group Plains of Fascination and Nellie contributed vocals to their album "Join the Ranks".

When Nellie graduated from Mount Douglas Secondary School, she returned to Toronto and formed Nelstar, a trio hop with Newkirk. Eventually, Nellie felt this style of music did not represent her personality nor allowed her to showcase her vocal ability. She left the group and decided to move back to Victoria.

Before going home, she performed at the 1997 Honey Jam, an all-female urban talent show. Her performance attracted the interest of The Philosopher Kings' singer Gerald Eaton, who approached her to write with him. Eaton and fellow Kings' member, Brian West, helped Nellie to produce her first demo.

The trio recorded material that led to her 1999 record deal with Dreamworks Records. They worked together on her debut album, "Whoa Nellie", which was released in October 2000. This album was an international success and received four Grammy Nominations in 2002. Her debut single, "I'm Like a Bird", won her a Grammy for Best Female Pop Vocal.

In 2007, Nellie hosted and performed at the 2007 Juno Awards in Saskatoon, Saskatchewan. At this event, Nellie won all five awards for which she was nominated. Her album "Loose" was a great success.

Nellie has also had a taste of acting as well. When she was young, she acted in many school plays. As an adult, she made guest appearances in an episode of CSI: New York and the daytime soap opera, One Life to Live.

Nellie's continuing experimentation with different instruments, sounds, genres, languages and vocal styles will more than likely increase and maintain her fame and success in the industry. ★

Nellie Furtado

Name: _____ Date: _____

Reading Skills

Circle the word that accurately completes each sentence. Record the word on the line.

1. Nellie's parents named her after a famous _____

   (singer, actor, gymnast, skater)

2. She first sang in her parents' native language _____

   (Russian, Spanish, Irish, Portuguese)

3. Nellie is able to play _____ instruments well.

   (three, five, seven, four)

4. In 1997, Nellie performed in a talent show called _____.

   (Star Search, Rising Star, Honey Jam)

5. In 2007, at the _____ Awards, Nellie won five awards.

   (Grammy, Juno, British, European)

Classify each statement as true or false.

6. Nellie Furtado claims her strong work ethic comes from her parents. _____

7. At the 2002 Grammy Awards, she won four awards. _____

8. Nellie went to Toronto to learn about and how to write classical music. _____

9. Nellie hosted and performed at the 2007 Juno Awards. _____

10. Her first album, "Whoa Nellie", was a great success. _____

Vocabulary Skills

Underline the word in each group that doesn't belong.

1. Portuguese, Russian, Polish, Italy
2. trombone, guitar, trumpet, tuba
3. work, labour, relax, toil
4. duet, single, trio, quartet
5. cultures, societies, peoples, teams

Using the dictionary, locate the meanings of the following words. Record the meaning used in the biography.

6. ethics: _____
7. contributed: _____
8. showcase: _____
9. nominated: _____
10. episode: _____

Research Skills

Using a world map to locate Portugal.

Using an encyclopedia or the internet, research to find out five interesting facts about this country.

_____
_____
_____
_____
_____

Quebec's Best Kept Secret — ★ Céline Dion ★

In a small Quebec town called Charlemagne, Céline Marie Claudette Dion was born on March 20, 1968. She was the youngest of 14 children and was raised in a poor but very happy home. Her parents, who were musicians, owned a small piano bar in the town and on weekends the entire family performed to entertain the customers. Céline began singing with her siblings at the tender age of five.

Céline dreamed of becoming a performer and at the age of 12, with the help of her mother and brother Jacques, she composed a French song which changed the course of her life. Her brother Michel sent the demo tape of her song "It Was Only a Dream," to a music manager named René Angélil. He was impressed with Céline's voice and song and decided to make her a star. He mortgaged his house to finance her debut album called "La voix du bon Dieu" (The Voice of God), which made Céline an instant star in Quebec.

Her popularity grew in Europe when she won the gold medal at the Yamaha World Song Festival as well as the coveted Musician's Award for Top Performer in 1982. In 1983, Céline became the first Canadian to ever receive a Gold Record in France.

By 1988, she had established a very strong fan base in her native province and was enjoying superstar status receiving many awards. In the same year, she won the prestigious European Song Contest in Dublin, Ireland where she performed in front of a television audience of 600 million viewers from European and Asian countries.

At 18, after seeing Michael Jackson perform, Céline told René that she wanted to be a star like him. He realized that her image needed to be changed in order for her to be marketed worldwide. For a number of months, Céline underwent a physical makeover and was sent to a special school to polish up her English. A year later, Céline made her first English album called "Unison".

Céline's international breakthrough came when she recorded the title song for the sound track of the animated movie "Beauty and the Beast." This song skyrocketed to number one and brought her an Academy and Grammy Award. Her second album simply called "Céline Dion" won an incredible number of Juno Awards. Another album called "Let's Talk About Love," which contained the theme song "My Heart Will Go On" from the movie "Titianic," sold millions of copies and won her a second Academy Award.

Céline and René, who was her manager and 26 years her senior, were secretly in love. This fact was hidden from the public in fear her fans would object to their feelings. However, in 1994, they decided to get married in Montreal on December 17. Their spectacular wedding was televised for all to see and her fans embraced it. After working at a breakneck pace for several years, Céline gave her last public appearance in Montreal on New Year's Eve in 1999 to begin a much needed break to enjoy her private life. During this break in 2001, she gave birth to a son called René-Charles who is one of the greatest joys in her life. In March of 2005, Céline returned to the musical world to perform five nights a week at the Colosseum at Caesar's Palace in Las Vegas for several years. With each new release, Céline has managed to top her previous successes and along the way has become one of the brightest stars in the world of popular music. ★

Céline Dion

Name: _____ Date: _____

Reading Skills

Record when each event took place in Céline Dion's life on the line provided.

1. first Canadian to win a gold record in France
_____

2. wanted to be a star like Michael Jackson
_____

3. won a gold medal at an important singing contest
_____

4. began singing in her parents' bar
_____

5. married her manager in a spectacular wedding
_____

6. won an important singing contest in Dublin, Ireland
_____

7. became a popular superstar in Quebec
_____

8. wrote a song that changed her life
_____

9. began performing in Las Vegas
_____

10. gave birth to a son named René-Charles
_____

Vocabulary Skills

Record synonyms found in the biography for the following words on the lines provided.

1. wrote _____
2. path _____
3. fame _____
4. appearance _____
5. viewers _____
6. important _____
7. unbelievable _____
8. very fast _____

Record antonyms found in the biography for the following words on the lines provided.

9. narrow _____
10. darkest _____
11. death _____
12. oldest _____
13. large _____
14. weak _____
15. earlier _____
16. front _____

A Musician With Heart ★ Sarah McLachlan ★

Since her debut in 1988, Sarah McLachlan's folk-pop sound has gained a devoted following of fans in Canada, the United States and the United Kingdom. She is an eight-time Juno Award winning and a three time Grammy Award winning Canadian musician, singer, and songwriter. Sarah is well known for the emotional sound of her ballads such as "Angel," "Building a Mystery," and "World on Fire." Her best-selling album to date is called "Surfacing" for which she won four Juno Awards and two Grammy Awards. It sold over 11 million copies worldwide and brought her much international success. Each album that Sarah has recorded demonstrates her continued growth as a singer and songwriter.

Sarah was born on January 28, 1968 and was adopted by Jack and Dorice McLachlan in Halifax, Nova Scotia. She also has two brothers named Stewart and Ian. Sarah began singing at the age of four. She learned to play the ukelele, the piano and the guitar, and took vocal lessons to develop her voice.

While in high school, Sarah was involved with a short-lived rock band called "The October Game." During her first year of college, the band opened for "Moev," an electronic music group specializing in synthpop. One of the members, Mark Jowett, was impressed with Sarah's singing and offered her a contract with his recording company, Nettwerk Records. Her parents convinced her to continue her studies at the Nova Scotia College of Art and Design before she began her new life as a recording artist. Two years later, she signed with Nettwerk Records and moved to Vancouver, British Columbia where the company was based.

In 1988, Sara recorded the first of her many albums "Touch," which achieved gold status in Canada. Her second album, "Solace," released in 1991, was a huge success in Canada and received some recognition from the United States. Sarah's third album, "Fumbling Towards

Ecstasy," in 1994 became her international break-through and scaled the charts in many countries. In 1997, Sarah recorded "Surfacing" which has been her best selling album.

One of her creative ventures was the organization of the "Lilith Fair" tour. This touring fair was the most successful all-female music festival in history. It brought together two million people over its three year history (1997-1999), raised more than seven million dollars for charities, and helped to launch the careers of several well-known female artists. Many artists such as the Indigo Girls, Sheryl Crow, Queen Latifah, Nellie Furtado, and Christine Aguilera participated in the tour.

For this creative endeavour, Sarah was awarded the Elizabeth Cady Stanton Visionary Award in 1998 for advancing the careers of women in music. In 1999, she was appointed as an Officer of the Order of Canada in recognition of her successful recording career, her role in Lilith Fair, and the charitable donations she made to women's shelters across Canada. In 2001, she was inducted to the Order of British Columbia. Sarah also funds a music educational program in Vancouver for inner city children.

During her busy career, Sarah found time to marry her long-time drummer Ashwin Sood in Negrel, Jamaica and have two little girls. ★

Sarah McLachlan

Name: _____ Date: _____

Reading Skills

Classify the following statements as *true* or *false*.

1. Sarah McLachlan has never won an Academy Award for her music.
   _____

2. The Lilith Fair tour was made up of well-known female and male Canadian artists.
   _____

3. Sarah McLachlan was the only child of Jack and Dorice McLachlan.
   _____

4. Sarah's parents wanted her to complete her education before becoming a recording artist.
   _____

5. Sarah's album "Touch" earned her two Grammy Awards and four Juno Awards.
   _____

6. Her best selling album is called "Surfacing."
   _____

7. Sarah works hard to improve her music with each album she records.
   _____

8. The first time Nettwerk Records offered her a contract, Sarah moved to Vancouver, British Columbia.
   _____

9. Many rewards and honours have been given to Sarah for her music and her generosity.
   _____

10. Sarah received international recognition with her album "Solace."
    _____

Vocabulary Skills

Record the *root word* for the following words on the line provided.

1. surfacing _____
2. specializing _____
3. copies _____
4. fumbling _____
5. organization _____
6. recognition _____
7. educational _____
8. charities _____

Join each word to its meaning with a line.

9. devoted •   • climbed
10. ballad •   • attempt
11. recognition •   • generous
12. scaled •   • loyal
13. endeavour •   • song
14. charitable •   • honour

A Piano Prodigy ☆ Chantal Kreviazuk ☆

Chantal Kreviazuk is the third child and only daughter of Jon and Carole Kreviazuk. She was born on May 18, 1973 in Winnipeg, Manitoba. She was raised in a wealthy suburb of Winnipeg along with two brothers who considered her the bratty little sister. When she was a little girl, Chantal would watch her brothers as they struggled through piano practice, hating every minute of it. She also wanted to play the piano but her mother felt she was too young. One day, her mother caught Chantal playing tunes on the piano and was amazed with her talent. She had a very good ear for music. Her mother soon arranged for her to take lessons.

Chantal trained in classical piano and voice at the Royal Conservatory of Music for many years. She competed in various festivals and competitions vocally and on the piano. During her teens in a fit of rebellion, Chantal quit the conservatory and gave up on the idea of becoming a classical concert pianist and formed a garage band with four boys. During this period in her life, Chantal began writing commercial jingles for money or playing the odd show on the lounge circuit. Songwriting was her escape from the pressures of adolescence as she felt self-conscious and unpopular and found her teen years horrible ones.

In September of 1994, Chantal was to begin studying at the University of Manitoba but never made it. During the summer she had been travelling through Europe with her then boyfriend. One day he suggested that they rent mopeds in order to see Florence, Italy better. While driving in the city that evening, Chantal accidentally drove her moped down a one way street. Suddenly she realized there was a motorcycle without its headlights on coming towards her, but it was too late to stop or get out of the way. Chantal was thrown off the moped during the impact. Her leg was broken and she had contusions all over her head. She spent three weeks in a foreign hospital in order to have reconstructive surgery on her face and leg. Once home in Winnipeg, Chantal was confined to her bed and was unable to move. At 21, she could not do the daily tasks such as having a bath and eating. In order to eat, she had to use a popsicle stick to open her mouth as she had six plates and twenty screws in her face.

During her long convalescence, Chantal had time to evaluate her life and to get her priorities in order. She realized that she had to take her music in a much more serious manner. It was something that she could give rather than use to get money. While she was ill, Chantal would sit at the piano and write songs. During this time period, Chantal recorded demos which were sent to various music studios. The head talent scout for Sony Records Canada heard her tape and was very impressed and immediately called Sony Music's president. Both men flew to Winnipeg the next day and offered her a contract for one million dollars for two albums over the next five years. Chantal was then flown to Los Angeles to begin recording her debut album called "Under These Rocks and Stones." This album and two of its singles gave Chantal her first Juno nomination as Best New Artist in 1997. For her second album, entitled "Colour Moving and Still," Chantal teamed up with Raine Maida, the lead singer of Our Lady Peace, to write songs. During that year, Chantal performed at the Juno Awards her single "Before You" and also won two awards for Best Adult/Pop Album and Best Female Artist.

In December of 1999, Chantal and Raine were married. Together, they have produced several albums and have written many songs. Chantal's work is often heard on many soundtracks for films and television shows. Since 2003, Chantal and Raine have written songs for other artists such as Avril Lavigne and Kelly Clarkson. Each year, the results of Chantal's work steadily improves and her fans readily await her new releases. ☆

Chantal Kreviazuk

Name: _____ Date: _____

Reading Skills

Number the events of Chantal's life in the correct order.

____ She wrote commercial jingles and played in lounges to make money.

____ During her convalescence, she spent time writing songs and making demos that were sent to various music studios.

____ As a child, Chantal wanted to play the piano like her brothers but her mother felt she was too young.

____ During a visit to Florence, Italy, Chantal was hit by a motorcycle while she was on a moped.

____ In December of 1999, Chantal married Raine Maida and together they have produced albums and written songs.

____ Chantal's mother realized her daughter was talented when she heard her playing tunes without any lessons.

____ In the summer of 1994, Chantal travelled about Europe with her boyfriend.

____ For many years, Chantal trained to become a classical pianist and vocalist at the Royal Conservatory of Music.

____ She was thrown off the moped and the impact broke her leg and badly damaged her face.

____ In her teens, Chantal gave up the idea of becoming a classical pianist.

____ Chantal was offered a contract by Sony Music Canada who flew her to Los Angeles to make her debut album.

Vocabulary Skills

Identify the part of speech that is underlined in each group of words. Record its name on the line provided.

1. in a <u>wealthy</u> suburb _____
2. bratty, little <u>sister</u> _____
3. <u>play</u> the piano _____
4. <u>classical</u> piano and voice _____
5. Chantal <u>accidentally</u> drove _____
6. in a <u>foreign</u> hospital _____
7. <u>to get money</u> _____
8. <u>produced</u> several albums _____

Locate an *antonym* for each word in the biography. Record the word on the line provided.

9. adult _____
10. died _____
11. poor _____
12. pleasant _____
13. away _____
14. morning _____

Add the endings *s, ed,* and *ing* to each word.

15. raise
   _____

16. struggle
   _____

17. travel
   _____

18. marry
   _____

Brash and Beautiful

★ Jully Black ★

Jully Black is a consistent figure in Canada's music scene and is one of the Rhythm and Blues pioneers to emerge out of Canada onto the international stage. Jully was born on November 8,1977 in Toronto, Ontario, and was named Jully Ann Inderia Gordon, and is of Jamaican heritage. She was raised in a single-parent household and is the youngest of nine children. Jully grew up in a notorious neighbourhood around the Jane and Finch Street area of Toronto known for its gangs, drugs and violence.

At the age of seven, Jully discovered she could sing while she participated in a church choir. At first, she was self-conscious, with her powerful alto range, as most people think if you have a high singing voice that you sing better. Jully worked on her alto voice and developed a smoothness with a raspy effect which makes her sound different from others and stand out. While she was growing up, music helped her to survive and she credits her success to her hard-working mother who continually inspired and encouraged Jully to work hard on her singing career. Jully was able to attend a school in Toronto to learn about other genres of music in a special music program, often having to travel by bus, subway train, or street car to get there.

Jully's fans admire her fearlessness and never holding back style while she performs on stage. Her husky, soul-stirring voice captured the attention of various rappers who recruited Jully to sing and write on their singles. Working with Canada's hip-hop elite became a launching pad and training ground for her career. Jully learned to write melodies and lyrics on the spot, how to perform in music videos, carry live performances and how to prepare for the spotlight. Her incredible ability to understand song structure, melody and expressive lyrics was noticed by Warner/Chappell Music, which signed her to a publishing contract at the age of 20.

Jully began to write her own songs as well as songs for international superstars such as

Destiny's Child, Nas and Esthero. She loves to perform as well, and has opened for singing greats such as Etta James, Anitia Baker, James Brown and Lauryn Hill. Jully has recorded many singles and three albums during her career. In 2003, her debut album, "I Travelled," was scheduled to be released by MCA Records but the company folded and her album was shelved. This was a major setback for Jully, but she picked herself up and started over. In 2005, a newly recorded album, "This is Me," was released by Universal Music Canada. Her second album "Rival," was released in 2007 and was awarded the Juno for Rhythm and Blues/Soul Recording of the Year in Calgary, Alberta in 2008 at the Juno Awards.

Jully is now a Celebrity Reporter on the television show eTalk and interviews popular movie and music stars. She also starred in the theatre production and TV series "Da Kink in my Hair." In 2008, Jully was thrilled when she was asked to be on Canadian Idol to act as a mentor, confidant, critic and coach to Idol competitors. Her passion, enthusiasm and love for music will surely be a fine example for the young musicians. ★

Jully Black

Name: _____ Date: _____

Reading Skills

Answer each question with a complete sentence. Record the sentence on the lines provided.

1. What music genre is Jully Black's speciality?
   _____
   _____
   _____

2. In what type of neighbourhood was Jully raised?
   _____
   _____
   _____

3. Why was Jully Black self-conscious of her alto singing voice?
   _____
   _____
   _____

4. As well as singing, in what other areas is Jully Black talented?
   _____
   _____
   _____

5. Why is Jully Black a good role model for other young musicians?
   _____
   _____
   _____

6. Why does Jully Black's voice stand out from other singers?
   _____
   _____
   _____

7. List the important skills Jully developed from working with the hip-hop elite?
   _____
   _____
   _____

Vocabulary Skills

Write each sentence below correctly by putting in the missing capital letters and the correct punctuation.

1. universal music canada released jully black's album entitled this is me in 2007
   _____
   _____
   _____

2. did you know that jully black is a celebrity reporter on the television show called e-talk
   _____
   _____
   _____

3. its a huge honour to have been asked to join canadian idol in 2008 said black during a interview
   _____
   _____
   _____

4. i am the youngest of nine children who were raised by a single mother in one of the worst areas in toronto said jully black to the student audience
   _____
   _____
   _____
   _____

Match the word to its meaning with a line.

5. genre •   • grating, harsh, rough
6. notorious •   • a very strong feeling
7. raspy •   • the words for a song
8. fearlessness •   • kind, sort, style
9. passion •   • afraid of nothing, daring
10. lyrics •   • having a bad reputation

A Punk Rocker — ★ Bif Naked ★

Bif Naked and her band have rocked in clubs and theatres in cities across North America as well as famous cities in Europe, such as Berlin, Paris, London, Milan, Barcelona, Madrid, Stockholm and Helsinki. She is famous for her quirky wit, distinctive vocal style and charm that make her quite unique.

Bif's birth name was Beth Torbert and she was born in New Delhi, India on June 15, 1971. She was adopted by two American missionaries who took her to Gettysburg, South Dakota, to Lexington, Kentucky, to Minneapolis, Minnesota and finally to Winnipeg, Manitoba, Canada. Her father was a professor of dentistry and taught at various universities in Canada and the United States.

At the age of 13 and sick of moving about, Bif began to rebel and traded in her ballet shoes for a skateboard and began hanging out at local arcades and skateboarding on the streets. She was a huge fan of Madonna and had dreams of becoming a star. After graduating from high school, Bif enrolled at the University of Winnipeg as a theatre major. During her first year, Bif joined her first band called Jungle Milk, which was a local group. Shortly after joining the band, she married the drummer who was also a member of another local group called Gorilla, Gorilla. When the lead singer from Gorilla, Gorilla quit on the eve of an important gig, Bif stepped in to take over the vocal duties. At the same time, she decided to invent a new name for herself. She chose her old high school nickname "Bif" as her first name and "Naked" as a last name because it was very punk rock sounding.

Bif was a natural at singing right from the beginning and the group began accumulating more fans as they toured. Life on the road took a toll on Bif. Her marriage ended in divorce after six months, and she had developed unhealthy habits which affected her

health, judgement and ability to make the right decisions.

After leaving Gorilla, Gorilla, Bif worked with two other bands called Chrome Dogs and Dying to be Violent. Finally, Bif decided to go out on her own in order to escape the boundaries put on her lyric writing by members in the bands and to put aside her punk rock lifestyle with all of her destructive activities. She gave up drinking, smoking, drugs and eating red meat to become a vegan. At this stage in her life, Bif felt she had a social responsibility to set an example for the young audiences who were attending her performances. This change in her lifestyle increased the power and the passion of her performances.

In 1994, Bif released an independent EP entitled "Four Songs and a Poem" and in 1995, her self-titled debut album "Bif Naked." Since then Biff has recorded many singles, music videos, and other albums. She has performed with Snoop Dogg, Billy Idol, Dido, Sarah McLachan, Sheryl Crowe, Chrissie Hynde, Foo Fighters and many more. In 2007, Biff married Ian Walker, a sports wriiter for the Vancouver Sun, in a traditional church ceremony in Vancouver on September 29, 2007. ★

Bif Naked

Name: _____ Date: _____

Reading Skills

Record true or false on the line at the beginning of each statement.

_____ 1. Biff married the lead singer of a group called Chrome Dogs.

_____ 2. As a child, Biff enjoyed moving to and living in different cities.

_____ 3. Touring with a band or group from city to city is not always glamourous.

_____ 4. Celine Dion was Bif's singing idol.

_____ 5. Bif Naked developed some nasty habits while she toured with the different bands.

_____ 6. Setting an example for her young fans became very important to Bif.

_____ 7. The members of the band Jungle Milk invented Beth Torbert's new name.

_____ 8. Adopting a better life style improved Bif's performances.

_____ 9. Bif Naked was born in Lexington, Kentucky.

_____ 10. After Bif went out on her own, she gave up all of her bad habits.

Write three questions that you would like to ask Bif Naked during an interview.

_____
_____
_____
_____

Vocabulary Skills

1. **Locate and record ten proper nouns found in the biography. List them in the correct alphabetical order.**

_____ _____
_____ _____
_____ _____
_____ _____
_____ _____

2. **Locate and record four compound words found in the biography.**

_____ _____
_____ _____

3. **Locate a synonym from the biography for each of the following words. Record it on the line provided.**

teacher _____

rules _____

duty _____

night _____

gathering _____

shows _____

Research Skills

Bif Naked performed in many famous cities in Europe during tours. Using an atlas or the internet, locate the country in which each of the following cities are found.

Berlin _____   Paris _____

London _____   Milan _____

Barcelona _____   Madrid _____

Stockholm _____   Helsinki _____

Answer Key

Male Athletes

Wayne Gretzky (Page 6)
Reading Skills:
1. Answers will vary.
2. He was scrawny and little.
3. He constantly practised his skating, stick handling, and shooting skills.
4. Answers may vary. Possible Answers: Edmonton Oilers; played with great hockey stars; worked on a winning team for five years straight; became rich and famous
5. The team gathered at centre ice for a group photo after they had won the Stanley Cup.
6. He was traded to the L.A. Kings.
7. It would be the last time that Wayne would wear a Canadian Team sweater again in the NHL.
8. They were Bobby Orr, Phil Esposito, and Gordie Howe.
9. Answers will vary.

Vocabulary Skills:
A. 1. scrunch 2. scrimp 3. scroll 4. scrounge 5. scrabble 6. scribble 7. scribe 8. scramble 9. scraggly
B. 1. Wayne Gretzky perhaps lived the most famous childhood of any athlete.
2. When he was fourteen, Wayne decided to leave Brantford to play for the Toronto Nats because jealous players and parents made him unhappy.
3. Wayne's most memorable game was Game 2 versus the Soviet Union during the 1987 Canada Cup.

Kurt Browning (Page 8)
Reading Skills:
1. Opinion
2. Fact
3. Opinion
4. Opinion
5. Fact
6. Opinion
7. Fact
8. Opinion
9. Fact
10. Opinion
11. Opinion
12. Fact

Vocabulary Skills:
A. 1. Words that could be circled: small, amusing, athletic, quick, talented, humble, wiry, caring, energetic, hardworking, artistic, entertaining, classy, outgoing, happy
B. 1. pp 2. ll 3. ff 4. zz 5. ss 6. ss 7. ll 8. ll 9. nn 10. ll 11. tt 12. ll
C. 1. ai 2. ai 3. ou; oo 4. oo 5. oo 6. oa 7. ee 8. ea 9. ou 10. ou 11. ea 12. ea

Donovan Bailey (Page 10)
Reading Skills:
1. 1991
2. 1981
3. 1998
4. 2000
5. 1996
6. 1965
7. 1997
8. 1997
9. 2001
10. 1997
11. 1996
12. 1967

Vocabulary Skills:
1. surge 2. steriods 3. tarnish 4. rupture 5. resume 6. accumulate 7. consultant 8. emigrate 9. envision 10. heritage

Research Skills:
1. They are drugs used to help people.
2. They control inflammation in the body and control conditions such as asthma and lupus.
3. Anabolic steroids are synthetic hormones.
4. They can boost the body's ability to produce muscle and prevent muscle breakdown.
5. Athletes hope they will improve their ability to run faster, lift heavy weights, jump higher, and have more endurance.
6. Answers will vary.

Steve Nash (Page 12)
Reading Skills:
A. 1. before
2. after
3. during
4. while
5. during
6. while
7. after
8. after
9. while
10. during
B. passionate, tall and skinny, committed, strong work ethics, thinker, undersized, dedicated, fearless, polished, team player

Vocabulary Skills:
A. 1. adage 2. illness 3. coveted 4. fearless 5. occasions 6. analyze 7. foster 8. stature 9. plagued 10. constantly 11. avid 12. spindly
B. Answers will vary.

Bobby Orr (Page 14)
Reading Skills:
1. His coach changed him from a forward to a defenceman.

2. They noticed the way he dominated the ice and his aggressive style of playing.
3. dominated the ice; rapid acceleration; control; physical style; defensive; fluid skating ability; end to end rushing
4. It impressed and excited them.
5. He began to have problems during his first season with the Bruins.
6. They felt that his body was not prepared for the physical abuse.
7. Answers will vary.
8. the first player to receive a large salary; changed the profile of a defenceman; dominated the game; made plays from the blue line

Vocabulary Skills:
A. 1. defensive 2. acceleration 3. dominate 4. fluid
   5. aggressive 6. prominent 7. orchestrated
   8. revolutionize 9. ambassador
B. 1. (A) 2. (S) 3. (S) 4. (A) 5. (A) 6. (S) 7. (S) 8. (A)
C. 1. (3) 2. (5) 3. (4) 4. (3) 5. (4) 6. (5) 7. (1) 8. (3)

Lennox Lewis (Page 16)
Reading Skills:
1. who, what, how many
2. who, where, why
3. who, what, when, where
4. when, who, how
5. how, why, who, where
6. who, when, how
7. who, what, how many
8. who, where, when, why
9. who, what

Vocabulary Skills:
1. bout 2. glass jaw 3. palooka 4. clinch 5. to take a dive
6. combination 7. down for the count 8. hook 9. southpaw
10. saved by the bell 11. draw 12. jab 13. breadbasket
14. sucker punch 15. gate

Alex Baumann (Page 18)
Reading Skills:
1. Czech Republic, New Zealand
2. three
3. Sudbury
4. 38
5. 2 gold
6. tense, nervous
7. Indiana
8. April
9. 72
10. 1912

Vocabulary Skills:
A. 1. tension 2. cerebral 3. tragedy 4. chronic 5. medley
   6. category 7. integrate 8. temporary 9. preceded
B. Answers will vary.

Female Athletes
Cindy Klassen (Page 20)
Reading Skills:
1. Her goal was to play on
2. Things were moving along as she
3. Her parents encouraged her to take
4. When Cindy was younger, she and
5. Much to her surprise, Cindy found
6. In a year, Cindy was on
7. While rounding a corner, Cindy crashed
8. Everyone felt that Cindy's skating season
9. Cindy Klassen will go down in

Vocabulary Skills:
A. 1. negative, positive 2. easy, difficult 3. happy, depressed
   4. strong, weak 5. most, least
B. Possible Answers: energetic, avid athlete, courageous, fearless, able to focus, positive, goal oriented, determined, successful, hardworking, thinker, fighter

Research Skills: Answers will vary.

Chantal Petitclerc (Page 22)
Reading Skills:
1. paralyzed, barn, door
2. swimming, strength, stamina
3. homemade, wheelchair
4. sprints, marathons
5. Barcelona, two, bronze
6. Paralympic, United States, gold, silver
7. Sydney, two, silver
8. Athens, Beijing, gold
9. athlete, social, history
10. role, model

Vocabulary Skills:
A. 1. remarkable 2. hardest 3. trailing 4. international
   5. swimming 6. recovery 7. specialist 8. successful
B. 1. par - a - lyzed 2. in - ter - view 3. com - pet - i - tor
   4. de - ter - min - a - tion 5. in - di - vid - u - al
   6. mar - a - thons
C. 1. waist, wheelchair, where, won, world
   2. farm, first, former, friends, future
   3. specialist, sports, stamina, status, strength
   4. many, marathons, medals, meter, middle
   5. career, coach, collection, competed, competitors

Perdita Felicien (Page 24)
Reading Skills:
1. She began at Pineridge Secondary School in Pickering.
2. She won the Ontario High School Hurdling Championships in 1997 and 1998.
3. She won the Canadian Junior Championships in hurdling.
4. She had several athletic scholarships offered to her by various universities.
5. She chose the University of Illinois and she studied Kinesiology.
6. Kinesiology is the science of how the body functions and moves. Answers will vary.

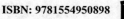

7. She won gold at the hurdling event at the World Championships.
8. She failed to clear a hurdle and crashed into an athlete in the adjacent lane.
9. Answers will vary.

Vocabulary Skills:

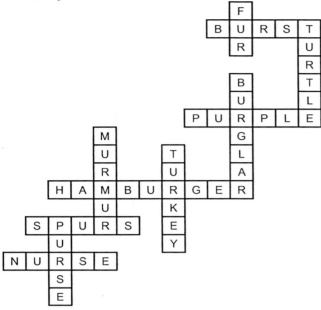

Research Skills:
Answers will vary. Possible Answers: rhythmic pattern, speed, elongated sprint stride, good technique, mobility, poise, stamina, long legs, strength

Beckie Scott (Page 26)
Reading Skills:
1. at the age of 13 or when a new coach came to town
2. Torino Olympics in 2006
3. at the age of 5
4. Salt Lake City Olympic Games in 2002
5. at the Junior National Championships
6. Olympic Games in Nagano, 1998
7. two and a half years later
8. Salt Lake City Olympics in 2002
9. in June of 2003
10. at the age of 7

Vocabulary Skills:
A. 1. brilliant 2. active 3. potential 4. succeed 5. fair
   6. positive 7. donate 8. maid
B. Answers will vary.

Research Skills: Answers will vary.

Hayley Wickenheiser (Page 28)
Reading Skills:
Sequential Order: 4, 8, 3, 1, 11, 7, 2, 6, 10, 5, 9

Vocabulary Skills:
A. 1. (A) 2. (S) 3. (A) 4. (S) 5. (H) 6. (H) 7. (A) 8. (A)
   9. (S) 10. (S)

B. 1. role 2. beat 3. thyme 4. team 5. bean 6. teem
   7. beet 8. been 9. roll 10. time

Beth Underhill (Page 30)
Reading Skills:
1. In show jumping, women are equal to men and the athlete competes with a horse as a partner.
2. The rider spends hours getting to know the personality of the horse and how it likes to work.
3. Answers may vary. Possible answers: A rider must have patience, persistence, control, good work ethics, knowledge, training and leadership.
4. They won over one million dollars at different events and Monopoly was popular in the show jumping world.
5. She became a sponsored rider for various owners.
6. The horse was called Altair.
7. She had investors buy Altair and brought him to Canada so she could ride him.
8. Answers will vary.

Vocabulary Skills:
A. 1. persistence 2. equine 3. personality 4. equestrian
   5. thoroughbred 6. eventing 7. intrigued 8. accuracy
   9. victorious 10. approach 11. dressage 12. investor
B. 1. expensive 2. mare 3. richest 4. warm 5. huge
   6. wrong 7. different 8. lady

Karen Cockburn (Page 32)
Reading Skills:
1. She is able to land flips exactly where she wants them on the trampoline.
2. Karen has a strong competitive drive that gives her the energy to perform difficult routines.
3. She used a trampoline during her training in diving.
4. Answers will vary.
5. She is part of a women's synchronized trampoline team.
6. They have won eight world cups in a row and captured gold at the 2007 World Championships.
7. She has won nine national titles, an Olympic bronze, two Olympic silver medals and dozens of World Cup medals.
8. She carried the Canadian flag during the closing ceremonies.

Vocabulary Skills:
A. 1. (3) 2. (5) 3. (3) 4. (4) 5. (4) 6. (4) 7. (4) 8. (3) 9. (4)
   10. (3)
B. 1. legend 2. trampoline 3. surgery 4. simulate
   5. synchronized 6. biography 7. reconstructive
   8. seriously

Research Skills:
1. George Nissen
2. He watched trapeze artists bouncing into somersaults and other moves in the safety netting.
3. Must take off and land with either their feet, seat, front, or back. Moves must be performed in 3 basic shapes: tucked, piked or straight.

Male Actors

Mike Myers (Page 34)
Reading Skills:
1. before 2. during 3. after 4. during 5. after 6. during
7. before 8. before 9. after 10. during

Vocabulary Skills:
A. 1. thrill 2. critic 3. animated 4. immersed
5. monumental 6. culture 7. adapted 8. natural
9. response

B. 1. (3) com - mer - cials
2. (4) en - ter - tain - ment
3. (4) mon - u - men - tal
4. (3) pres - ti - gious
5. (4) an - i - mat - ed
6. (5) i - mag - i - na - tion
7. (4) co - me - di - an
8. (3) neg - a - tive

Ryan Gosling (Page 36)
Reading Skills:
1. Remember the Titans
2. Frankenstein and Me
3. Breaker High
4. The Believer
5. Murder by Numbers
6. Half Nelson
7. Fracture
8. The Slaughter Rule
9. Young Hercules
10. The Notebook
11. Mickey Mouse Club
12. Stay

Vocabulary Skills:
A. 1. attractive 2. ambitious 3. charming 4. compelling
5. integrations 6. impressive 7. foundling
8. hypochondriac 9. outwit 10. thriller 11. whim
12. revival

B. 1. oldest 2. learn 3. life 4. smooth 5. set 6. dull
7. past

Michael J. Fox (Page 38)
Reading Skills:
1. He dreamed about becoming a hockey player.
2. He quit school before he graduated.
3. He couldn't register it with the Screen Actors' Guild because it was the same as another actor's name.
4. He spent money freely and got into debt and had to sell his possessions.
5. He played Alex P. Keaton in the television series "Family Ties"
6. He won four awards for his acting ability.
7. While he was shooting a movie he noticed his little finger quivering.
8. It is called young on-set Parkinson's Disease.
9. He kept his hand in his pocket.
10. He would like to find a cure for Parkinson's Disease.

Vocabulary Skills:
A. 1. debilitate 2. reference 3. symptom 4. register
5. prominent 6. veteran 7. triology 8. guild
9. pursue 10. duplicate

Research Skills: Answers will vary.

Matthew Perry (Page 40)
Reading Skills:
1. Ottawa
2. Massachusetts
3. tennis
4. friends
5. comedy
6. Fools Rush In
7. attorney
8. Chandler Bing
9. ten
10. fifteen

Vocabulary Skills:
A. 1. divorced 2. nightmare 3. amateur 4. tragedy
5. follow 6. enemies 7. finished 8. senior

B. 1. lifted 2. found 3. registering 4. primarily
5. difficulties 6. throw 7. endured 8. lawyer
9. hardest

Jim Carrey (Page 42)
Reading Skills:
1. How the Grinch Stole Christmas
2. Yuk Yuk's Comedy Club
3. in a yellow polyester suit with tails
4. The Comedy Store
5. Rodney Dangerfield
6. The Duck Factory
7. The Mask
8. a loveable numbskull
9. The Riddler
10. The Cable Guy

Vocabulary Skills:
A. 1. predecessor 2. numbskull 3. staple 4. polyester
5. manic 6. goofball 7. extrovert 8. marquee
9. outrageous

B. 1. phrase 2. verb 3. proper noun 4. adjectives
5. common nouns

Keanu Reeves (Page 44)
Reading Skills:
1. His mother divorced and married several times. He had several stepfathers. The family moved about frequently. He has no relationship with his birth father. Keanu was raised by a variety of caregivers.
2. He excelled in hockey.
3. He had a bad attitude and a disability called dyslexia.
4. He enjoyed playing in *Youngblood* because he played the role of a goalie.
5. It was in the movies *Bill & Ted's Excellent Adventure* and *Bill & Ted's Bogus Journey*.

6. Answers will vary.
7. Answers will vary.

Vocabulary Skills:
A. 1. mnemonic 2. prolific 3. geologist 4. unstable
   5. abandoned 6. rambunctious 7. academics
   8. dyslexia 9. desirable 10. advocate 11. matrix
   12. buffoon

Research Skills: Answers will vary.

Keifer Sutherland (Page 46)
Reading Skills:
1. he wanted to become an actor
2. he won awards and is the highest paid television star
3. his parents were actors working there
4. he inherited this ability from his parents, who are actors
5. he is his grandfather or grandson
6. he was broke
7. he had a bad boy look and suited the roles
8. he needed a break from acting and the films that he was making
9. he loved the discipline and the experience
10. he preferred to act in movies and on the stage.

Vocabulary Skills:
A. 1. a collection of wild animals kept on display
   2. pertaining to the theatre or dramatic performances
   3. having or exercising power
   4. to regulate under group or government control
   5. able to attract or influence others
   6. a soldier armed with a musket
   7. the result of an action or condition
   8. a break or interruption
   9. unlawful acts of violence
   10. one who acts or has the power to act
B. Three Syllable Words: theatrical, production, intentions, apartment
   Four Syllable Words: consequences, menagerie, terrorism, dissatisfied, influential
   Five Syllable Words: occasionally, experimenting, eventually

Female Actors

Sarah Polley (Page 48)
Reading Skills:
1. Straight Up
2. Lantern Hill
3. The Sweet Hereafter
4. Road to Avonlea
5. One Magic Christmas
6. Guinevere
7. Ramona
8. Almost Famous
9. The Road to Avonlea

Vocabulary Skills:
A. 1. perseverence; lasting 2. an English dialect
   3. extremely sad event 4. correspond to; similar
   5. life after death 6. a surrounded area 7. like no other
   8. extreme force; overpowering
B. 1. orphan 2. clash 3. rewarded 4. lantern
   5. impact 6. intelligent 7. prominent
   8. breakthrough
C. 1. fame 2. busy 3. act 4. persist
   5. finance 6. progress

Kim Cattrall (Page 50)
Reading Skills:
1. Porky's
2. Ticket to Heaven
3. City Limits
4. Mannequin
5. Star Trek VI: The Undiscovered Country
6. Ice Princess
7. Police Academy
8. The Incredible Hulk
9. Hold-Up
10. Big Trouble in Little China

Vocabulary Skills:
A. Sentences will vary.
B. 1. education, emigrated, engineer, executive
   2. signed, studied, studios, styles
   3. debut, die, director, dramatic
   4. magically, many, member, movie
   5. family, final, financial, finished

Neve Campbell (Page 52)
Reading Skills:
1. Her father took her to see The Nutcracker.
2. She inherited the ability from her father and grandparents.
3. She won a full scholarship to train with the National Ballet Company of Canada.
4. She studied six different types of dancing.
5. A dancer's body can suffer from many different kinds of injuries.
6. Dancing took a toll on her body and her mind.
7. The movie Scream was a box office success.
8. It was called The Company.

Vocabulary Skills:
A. Answers will vary for questions 1 to 5.
B. 1. custody 2. toll 3. flamenco 4. junction
   5. insight 6. bursitis 7. stadium
   8. tendonitis

Sandra Oh (Page 54)
Reading Skills:
1. Answers will vary. Possible answers are: involved with students' council; voted head girl or co-president of the high school; formed an environmental club called BASE
2. played volleyball, cross country skiing; involved in many extra curricular activities
3. on the school's honour roll; won a four year scholarship

4. did ballet dancing; involved in drama classes; acted in school plays; joined the school drama club; took part in the Canadian Improv Games and Skit Row High comedy group
5. Answers will vary.
6. Answers will vary.
7. Possible Answers: intelligent, creative, hardworking, considerate, determined, competitive, athletic, talented, wise, extrovert, successful, activist, caring, energetic, outgoing

Vocabulary Skills:
A. Sentences must all be questions.
B. Sentences must all be statements.

Wendy Crewson (Page 56)
Reading Skills:
1. 1990, Getting Married in Buffalo Jump
2. 1992, I'll Never Get to Heaven
3. 1993, The Good Son
4. 1998, From Earth to Moon
5. 1999, At the End of the Day: The Sue Rodriguez Story
6. 1999, Sleeping Dogs Lie
7. 1997, Air Force One
8. 2002, Hunt for Justice: The Louise Arbour Story
9. 2006, The Man Who Lost Himself
10. 2007, Away From Her

Vocabulary Skills:

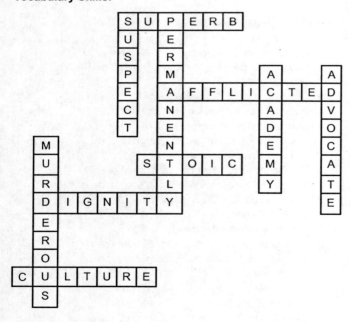

Anna Paquin (Page 58)
Reading Skills:
1. Canada
2. nine
3. cello, piano, viola
4. The Piano
5. can't talk
6. 5,000

7. surprise
8. Oscar
9. geese
10. United States, New Zealand

Vocabulary Skills:
A. 1. befell 2. cameo 3. remarkable 4. intentions
   5. tragedy 6. fluke 7. transition 8. impressive

Research Skills: Answers will vary

Meg Tilly (Page 60)
Reading Skills:
The statements that should be underlined are 2, 5, 7, 8, 10, and 11.

Vocabulary Skills:
A. 1. (A) 2. (S) 3. (S) 4. (H) 5. (S) 6. (A)
   7. (S) 8. (H) 9. (H) 10. (A)
B. 1. tense 2. thrill 3. flat 4. fortune
   5. serious 6. wise 7. million 8. mystery
   9. trash 10. union

Male Musicians

The Barenaked Ladies (Page 62)
Reading Skills:
1. Kevin Hearn 2. Andy Creeggan, Tyler Stewart
3. Ed Robertson, Steven Page 4. Andy Creeggan
5. Ed Robertson, Steven Page 6. Andy Creeggan
7. Ed Robertson 8. Jim Creeggan 9. Tyler Smith
10. Steven Page 11. Ed Robertson, Steven Page
12. Tyler Stewart, Kevin Hearn

Vocabulary Skills:
A. 1. playful teasing, joking
   2. made up on the spur of the moment
   3. what people think and say about a person
   4. period of ten years 5. duet 6. to add tones to a melody
B. 1. convention 2. harmony 3. converse 4. perform
   5. rehearse 6. misery 7. collect 8. nominate

Research Skills: South America

Kalan Porter (Page 64)
Reading Skills:
1. Kalan grew up on a 2. At the age of 16
3. SWASS also won first place
4. Kalan's mother claims he could
5. Kalan appeared as a very
6. During the competition, Kalan used
7. The ballard went on to
8. Answers will vary.

Vocabulary Skills:
A. 1. re/al/ity 2. Al/ber/ta 3. cor/ral/ling 4. pro/vinc/ial
   5. in/tel/li/gent 6. pas/sion/ate 7. au/di/tion
   8. com/pe/ti/tion
B. fundraisers, wakeboard, snowboard, volleyball
C. 1. real, true, sincere without pretense
   2. a wise and trusted advisor 3. forecast
   4. an instrument shaped like a violin

5. high quality music
6. a group of musicians used in a performance
7. interpretation of the meaning

Bryan Adams (Page 66)
Reading Skills:
True Statements are 2,4,5,7,8,10,12
Vocabulary Skills: Answers will vary.
Research Skills: Austria, Canada, England, France, Israel, Portugal, United States

Billy Talent (Page 68)
Reading Skills:
1. members, band, Mississauga
2. guitar, Dragonflower
3. Solowoniuk, disease, multiple sclerosis
4. Ben, radio, station
5. Pezz. Billy, Talent
6. pooled, money, demo, Dudebox
7. Junos, Group, Album
8. original, unique
9. released, length, recorded

Vocabulary Skills:
A. 1. one of a kind; unusual
   2. to cause to be swallowed up or absorbed so as to lose its own character or identity
   3. to try to equal or excel
   4. the preparation of an animated cartoon
B. 1. higher 2. full 3. different 4. success
C. 1. sound 2. record 3. began 4. merged

Research Skills: Answers will vary.

Sam Roberts (Page 70)
Reading Skills:
1. Opinion 2. Fact 3. Opinion 4. Opinion 5. Fact
6. Fact 7. Opinion 8. Fact 9. Opinion 10. Opinion

Vocabulary Skills:
A. 1. (A) 2. (S) 3. (A) 4. (H) 5. (A) 6. (H) 7. (A) 8. (A)
   9. (H) 10. (S) 11. (A) 12. (H) 13. (A) 14. (A)
B. Answers will vary but must demonstrate the meaning.

Brian Melo (Page 72)
Reading Skills:
1. fifth, talent
2. confidence, ability
3. praised, emotional, stage
4. immigrants, Portugal, Hamilton
5. private, secrets, parents
6. performance, stimulated, cheering
7. construction, vocalist, band
8. judges, audience, ovation
9. composers, lyricists, debut
10. supported, motivated, contest

Vocabulary Skills:
A. 1. the highest point 2. induced to act; to give incentive
   3. the fact or condition of being present in a place
   4. power to resist; sustain or recover from that which weakens
   5. so spur on; stir up 6. covered by a liquid
   7. to give an order or direction 8. special; like no other
B. 1. "Mr. and Mrs. Melo, your son may very well be the next Canadian Idol!" exclaimed Zack Werner excitedly.
   2. "I give every ounce of my heart and soul that I have to my loyal fans who have supported me throughout the Idol Competition," replied Brian Melo during an interview.

Sum 41 (Page 74)
Reading Skills:
1. high school
2. three
3. helped to make a documentary
4. Ajax, Ontario
5. Chuck Pelletier
6. Steve Jocz, Deryck Whibley, Jason McCaslan
7. Deryck Whibley
8. ate ice cream cones at lunch
9. Steve Jocz
10. ten million
11. 300 performances
12. Steve Jocz

Vocabulary Skills:
A. 1. peacekeeper 2. nickname 3. worldwide 4. lifestyle
   5. teenage 6. website 7. throughout 8. gunfire
B. 1. <u>document</u>ary 2. un<u>harm</u>ed 3. <u>label</u>led
   4. inter<u>nation</u>al 5. <u>glob</u>al 6. a<u>part</u>ment 7. <u>produc</u>er
   8. <u>current</u>ly

Research Skills: Answers will vary.

Female Musicians

Avril Lavigne (Page 76)
Reading Skills:
1. Belleville 2. two 3. Shania Twain 4. Complicated
5. Chapters bookstore 6. sixteen 7. gondola ride
8. four Junos

Vocabulary Skills:
1. complicated 2. scaled 3. escort 4. rapport 5. peer
6. con - ti - nent 7. pro - fes - sion - al
8. man - age - ment 9. videotapes, fairgrounds, bookstore, songwriter, throughout

Nellie Furtado (Page 78)
Reading Skills:
1. gymnast 2. Portuguese 3. four 4. Honey Jam
5. Juno 6. True 7. False 8. False 9. True 10. True

Vocabulary Skills:
1. Italy 2. guitar 3. relax 4. single 5. teams
6. have morals, honourable style of working
7. to help with work 8. to present's one's ability
9. suggest a name for a position 10. part of a serial story

Celine Dion (Page 80)
Reading Skills:
1. 1983 2. age 18 3. 1982 4. age 5 5. December 17, 1994
6. 1988 7. 1988 8. age 12 9. 2005 10. 2001
Vocabulary Skills:
1. composed 2. course 3. popularity 4. image
5. audience 6. prestigious 7. incredible 8. breakneck
9. wide 10. brightest 11. life 12. youngest 13. small
14. strong 15. later 16. back

Sarah McLachlan (Page 82)
Reading Skills:
1. True 2. False 3. False 4. True 5. False 6. True
7. True 8. False 9. True 10. False
Vocabulary Skills:
1. surface 2. special 3. copy 4. fumble 5. organize
6. recognize 7. educate 8. charity 9. devoted, loyal
10. ballad, song 11. recognition, honour 12. scaled, climbed
13. endeavour, attempt 14. charitable, generous

Chantal Kreviazuk (Page 84)
Reading Skills:
Sequence Order: 5, 9, 1, 7, 11, 2, 6, 3, 8, 4, 10
Vocabulary Skills:
1. adjective 2. noun 3. verb 4. adjective 5. adverb
6. adjective 7. phrase 8. verb 9. child 10. born
11. wealthy 12. horrible 13. towards 14. evening
15. raises, raised, raising 16. struggles, struggled, struggling
17. travels, travelled, travelling
18. marries, married, marrying

Jully Black (Page 86)
Reading Skills:
1. rhythm and blues
2. notorious one known for its drugs, gangs, and violence
3. everyone thinks a high voice sounds better
4. songwriting, interviewing stars, helping young musicians
5. Answers will vary.
6. smooth with a raspy or husky voice
7. able to write melodies and lyrics on the spot; how to perform in music videos; how to carry live performances; how to prepare for the spotlight
Vocabulary Skills:
1. **U**niversal **M**usic **C**anada released **J**ully **B**lack's album entitled **"T**his is **M**e**"** in 2007**.**
2. **D**id you know that **J**ully **B**lack is a **C**elebrity **R**eporter on the television show e-**T**alk**?**
3. **"**It's a huge honour to have been asked to join **C**anadian Idol in 2008**,"** said **B**lack during an interview**.**
4. **"**I am the youngest of nine children who were raised by a single mother in one of the worst areas in Toronto**,"** said **J**ully **B**lack to the student audience**.**
5. kind, sort or style 6. having a bad reputation
7. grating, harsh, rough 8. afraid of nothing, daring
9. a very strong feeling 10. the words of a song

Bif Naked (Page 88)
Reading Skills:
1. True 2. False 3. True 4. False 5. True 6. True
7. False 8. True 9. False 10. True
Vocabulary Skills:
1. Answers will vary.
2. lifestyle, skateboard, nickname, skateboarding
3. teacher - professor; rules - boundaries;
   duty - responsibility; night - eve; gathering - accumulating;
   shows - performances
Research Skills:
Berlin - Germany; Paris - France; London - England;
Milan - Italy; Barcelona - Spain; Madrid - Spain;
Stockholm - Sweden; Helsinki - Finland